BOUND FOR GLORY

BOUND FOR GLORY

GOD'S PROMISE FOR YOUR FAMILY

R. C. SPROUL, JR.

CROSSWAY BOOKS·

A DIVISION OF
GOOD NEWS PUBLISHERS
WHEATON, ILLINOIS

Bound for Glory

Copyright © 2003 by R. C. Sproul, Jr.

Published by Crossway Books
    A division of Good News Publishers
    1300 Crescent Street
    Wheaton, Illinois 60187

Cover design: Josh Dennis

Cover photo: Getty Images

First printing, 2003

Printed in the United States of America

Scripture quotations are taken from the Holy Bible: English Standard Version, copyright © 2001 by Crossway Bibles, a division of Good News Publishers, Wheaton, Illinois 60187.

Library of Congress Cataloging-in-Publication Data
Sproul, R. C. (Robert Craig), 1965-
    Bound for glory : God's promise for your family / R. C. Sproul, Jr.
    p. cm.
    ISBN 1-58134-495-3 (alk. paper)
    1. Family—Religious aspects—Christianity. I. Title
BV4526.3.S67   2003
248.4—dc21   2003003725

BP		13	12	11	10	09	08	07	06	05	04	03
15	14	13	12	11	10	9	8	7	6	5	4	3	2	1

To Denise,
my covenant woman

Contents

INTRODUCTION

I am the envy of many sons. While they may not even be aware of it, from time to time I see the green-eyed monster rear its ugly head when men ask me the single most common question I am asked: "What is it like to have R. C. Sproul as your father?" The question not only reveals a level of jealousy, however; it can demonstrate a misunderstanding of what really matters. Imagine, for example, that you lived in ancient Israel. The land is yet without a king, but God in His grace has provided Samuel to serve as judge over the land. Samuel, of course, is renowned across the nation for his godliness of character. As a prophet, people come to him seeking wisdom. God Himself speaks to Samuel. Now, would you ask Samuel's sons, with envy, "What is it like to have Samuel as your father?" I think not. Samuel, for all the great and mighty things he did for the kingdom of God, failed miserably to do the most important thing—raise godly children.

King David's renown far surpassed Samuel's, the one who anointed him. He not only served as a model of a godly king, but he was favored by God, who called him "a man after his own heart" (1 Samuel 13:14). Would you ask any of his many children, borne by his many wives, "What's it like to have

David as your father?" Of course not. For as David's service was more spectacular than Samuel's, so was his failure as a father.

Before you get too worried, the point of this is not to argue that while everyone thinks my father is such a great man, no one knows the agony I went through growing up. By no means. The point instead is that what makes my father a great man is not that he has a radio program, not that he writes books that thousands of people buy, not that he teaches at prestigious seminaries. Instead, what makes my father a great man is something that you don't get to see—he is a great father.

It would have been both easy and all too common for my father to look at his life, see the prospects before him, and devote himself to his strengths, to the neglect of his calling. He could go through his life enjoying the accolades that come with being a popular theologian and teacher. It would be all the more understandable for this reason: While his own father served as a wonderful model and teacher on how to be a wonderful father, those lessons ended when my father was only seventeen, when his father died. But my father understands what those who ask me about having him as a father too often miss—the kingdom of God is built not by writing best-selling books, but by raising up godly seed.

The true heroes of the faith, then, are not ultimately those whose books make the best-seller lists. Fidelity is not measured by a capacity to teach great crowds of people. And that ought, of course, to be good news for us all. We do not all have to have the ability to teach thousands of people. We do not all have to have doctorates or pulpits to do great things for the kingdom. All we have to do is raise up godly seed. (Of course, there are many other things we can do for the kingdom as well. But this book is about families.) If God has blessed us with a wife and children, we are already armed for the battle. We are ready to do great things for the kingdom.

My prayer is that this book will help. Its journey is somewhat unusual. What you are holding began as a radio program and a video series produced by my father's ministry, Ligonier Ministries. That series included not only a series of talks by me on the subject of the family, but also a series of talks by a family—conversations about the family between my father and me. One such conversation preceded the taping, and another came after. In like manner, we will begin this book with one conversation and end with another. In between it's just me. I think it is important to include these conversations in the book, not only for what is taught *in* those conversations, but for what is taught *by* them. My goal for the book is that we might be equipped to make manifest the reign of Christ in and through our families. My goals for including these conversations are these: First, I pray that you will learn something of the call of a son to honor his father. Second, I hope you will see the true greatness of my father— that he is a great father.

A FATHER AND SON CONVERSATION
In the dialogue that follows, the comments of the father (R. C. Sproul, Sr.) appear in roman type, those of the son (R. C. Sproul, Jr.) in italics.

Over thirty years ago when I was working at a church in Cincinnati I became close friends with a man who was a detective on the Cincinnati police force, and one of the things that was exciting to discover in my friendship with him was that he had become a Christian as a result of the direct influence of his son and his daughter. Both of his kids became Christians before he did, and as a result of their testimony in the home he came to Christ.

While I can't say that I became a Christian because of the influence of my children on my life, I do relate to my friend's experience back in Cincinnati in that I have been profoundly influenced and instructed on some very significant things about the Christian faith from my own children, certainly not the least of which is the influence I've had from my son, Dr. R. C. Sproul, Jr., particularly with respect to the covenant family.

When Ligonier Ministries decided to put together a teaching series on the family, and we talked about how to do it, one of the questions that came to me was, should I be the one to do that lecture series? I said, "Well, I could, if we want to have Ligonier's second-best do it." But since I really believe R. C., Jr. knows so much more about this subject than I do, I thought it would be much more fitting to have him do it. I know how biased parents can be and so on, but in all honesty I have never met anybody in my life who has displayed to me a commitment to training up their children in the things of God like R. C., Jr. I have witnessed what he does with my grandchildren, and it absolutely amazes me on the one hand and shames me on the other. When R. C. was a little boy, I prayed for him and his older sister constantly. I knew the biblical passage that says nobody has any greater joy than to see their children walking in the truth of the Lord. It was my great desire to see them grow up in the nurture and admonition of the Lord. We'll talk a little later about our experiences in our home, but we didn't come anywhere close to the discipline of training children as R. C. has done in his family. He has shown me so many things, I wanted to let everybody else have that opportunity.

But one other thing I want to say is that this week I've been listening on the radio to my friend Alistair Begg, and one of the lectures he gave was on the Hebrew *shema*. We're all aware, at least those of us who have Jewish friends, that they have a little scroll on their doorposts that contains the words of the *shema*: "Hear, O Israel: The LORD our God, the LORD is one. You shall love the LORD your God with all your heart and with all your soul and with all your might" (Deuteronomy 6:4-5). And then it goes on to give the mandate that God gives to the parents in Israel to speak of these things with their children when they rise up in the morning, when they go to bed at night, and so on, that in all circumstances the children may be taught by the parents. The tendency in our culture is to transfer the responsibility of training in godliness to the Christian school or to the church or Sunday school rather than seeing this mandate given to the parents by the Lord Himself. And so, R. C., I'm so glad that you are willing to do this series on the covenant family, and sort of to frame that, I'd like you to talk to me a little bit today about some of your experiences and our experiences as family.

Well, I think you were too hard on yourself this morning. I run the danger in my life as a man of coming to the Scriptures and saying, "What does the Word say I'm supposed to do as a man?" My temptation is to look to you and say to myself, "I love my father. My father's my hero. That's what I want to be," and not going beyond that.

It is indeed sad when men do that. I understand. I can feel your pain there. I've been trying to get you to call me your hero for thirty-five years, you know. But seriously, let me ask you a question, all right? When do you become a man?

When you say I'm a man.

When I say you're a man, okay.

And as I'm listening to you, I'm thinking, of course, about my own desire to be a godly husband and father and to make you proud. Before I came down here I spoke with my children, and I said, "Daddy's got to go do some work. Daddy's going to go and speak about the Christian family." And I said, "I want you to know why. The reason Daddy's going down to talk about the Christian family is because people know you." I said, "Your grandfather knows you, and your grandfather is so pleased with you that he thinks I can come talk to people about the family." I said, "You know that the Scripture says"—they know this because we studied Proverbs together—"that children can and should be a delight to their parents and bring honor to their parents." I said, "Daddy has honor because of you guys." I want to return the children to the Lord, to whom they belong, and say, "These are Yours, and I'm dependent upon You," and in a similar way I return them to my father. In this series we're going to talk about one of the things that we're missing. As Christians we look into the world, and we see the family is falling apart. Our vision is to defend the family; and our understanding of the family, because the world is so confused on the issue, is so narrow that what we need to do is get beyond the vision of the nuclear family and get back to a vision of patriarchy. This past weekend I was speaking at a conference put on by a friend who publishes a magazine called Patriarch.

I bet that's real popular today.

Well, you know, and I talked about this there as well, I want to be a faithful member of the Sproul clan, and you are the patriarch. My eldest is nine, but even though she's only nine, I'm telling all of my children, including her, "Look, there's going to come a day when you're going to be leaders in your homes." I tell my daughter, "You're going to have a husband, God willing," and I tell my son, "You're going to have a wife, God willing," and I tell them both, "You're going to have to be ready to lead your families." And it's a wonderful experience to be able to teach them. We home-school our children, and the last few weeks Denise and I (my wife, your daughter-in-law) have been working out schedules and what are we going to cover and when are we going to do it, and we've decided that twice a week I'm going to meet with my son and do Bible study with him. When he found that out, his face lit up, and his eyes turned to saucers. That whole week he kept telling me, "Four more days, Daddy." "Three more days, Daddy." And when we finally sat down, I began to talk about what it means to be the head of your home and began to talk to him about what I want him to do. I said, "You already have a realm over which you rule." One of his jobs is to feed the cats and the dogs and the chickens.

Oh my. You've entrusted those famous chickens to Campbell.

Yes, and that was a mistake.

I don't know. I would think they'd be faring as well as they were before.

That's the point. Won't I be embarrassed when he succeeds where I have failed! There is no place to go but up. He can't do any worse than I did. He does that, and he cleans the baseboards in the house. And I explained to him, "You know Daddy has given Mommy the responsibility and the authority to keep the house tidy and neat because you know what would happen if I did that, and she has now delegated to you the responsibility of these baseboards, and that's what I want you to do. This is your area of responsibility, and I want to see you do a good job."

You know, this is part of what we mean about talking about the statutes of the Lord when we rise up and when we lie down. My son has a chore—to clean the baseboards in the house, and I want to turn that into a lesson on what it means to be a godly man. That kind of thing is in many ways—you don't think so—but in many ways it is something that I learned from you. I mean, we were not homeschooled. I wish we had been, but in God's providence we weren't. But I doubt many parents were more involved than you were and who also, outside of the raw academics, took the time to teach the lessons.

Well you know, R. C., you talk about the patriarchal thing, and I have to say to you—I mean when you get choked up about looking to your father and so on, one of the greatest pains of my life is that you never met your grandfather. My father was my greatest hero, and there was no one in the world whom I wanted to please more than I wanted to please him. He died when I was seventeen years old, long, of course, before you were born. So you never had the opportunity to meet him.

Right.

But also you never had the opportunity to meet my grandfather, for whom we were both named. His name was R. C. also. He really was, in my experience, the patriarch. I never think of myself as being a patriarch. When I think of patriarchy in our family, I think of the one they called R. C., my grandfather. He was such a godly gentleman, and *gentleman* was the word that really captured him. He died when I was six years old, so you would think I wouldn't have many memories of my grandfather, but I have—I'm filled with memories of him. There was a lifelong impact on me from that man, from his model. I mean, I spent every Sunday afternoon with him from the time I was born until the time I was six years old, and in that small window of opportunity, he made an enormous impact on me. And then after he died, my father had that impact also; there was a sense in which I could see through my father to his father.

I understand that.

Do you?

Yes, I do.

Do you sort of feel like you know my father a little bit, even though you never met him?

Yes. As I was preparing for this particular series, I was thinking exactly that. I was thinking, I never met my grandfather, but I know that he was a great man of God, and I know that because of what you say about him, how you feel about him. I know you wouldn't have that deep and abiding love and respect for him if he hadn't been.

But it wasn't just my father and grandfather. As a boy growing up, on my father's side were my cousins, and I was the youngest one. I had all these older cousins.

You were precious.

Yeah, I was the precious one. I was the baby of the family, and our family was the kind that every Thanksgiving, every Christmas, every Easter, the whole family—because they all lived in the Pittsburgh area—gathered together for the day. And I also lived in an extended family. Growing up we had my father, my mother, my sister, and I, plus an uncle, an aunt, and their daughter, plus another uncle, plus another cousin, plus my grandmother all living under the same roof. We had twelve rooms in our house by the time my dad stopped adding on to accommodate all these family members that we had growing up. So talk about an extended family! And I was the youngest, of course. I was overwhelmed by all these people, and yet they were my favorite people in the world. My favorite days were those Easters and Thanksgivings and Christmases when the whole family got together. And to this day, those people who still are left are the most important people in my life. When it comes right down to it, you can have friends, and you can have acquaintances and buddies, co-laborers and all that, but as close as those relationships are and as meaningful as they are, to me there's nothing like family. And yet I talk to people all the time who are from so-called "broken" homes, "broken" families who don't have that sense of strong ties. What a terrible tragedy it is to have families that don't have the kind of bonding that I experienced. I look back at my home life, and I think I was extremely blessed. I was never abused. I was encouraged; I was disciplined; I was loved, and not just by my mother and father, but by my aunt who lived with us. I called her my step-mother-aunt, and when she died, it was like having my mother die. My cousin who lived in our house for ten years was ten years older than I am. She's not my cousin— she's my sister as far as I'm concerned. And it's a wonderful experience.

It certainly is, and it's a shaping experience, as you've just described. One of our weaknesses in our families today is we think that if we all live under the same roof, then that's all it takes; but it takes time and intentionality to build those bonds. And we miss that because we all have our separate lives.

Well, R. C., I know that you know that your mother loves you and that your father loves you and that your wife loves you and that your children love you and all of that, but I'll tell you one more thing—you live in Virginia, and your sister still lives in my house (she has for twenty years with her husband and their kids), but I want you to know, your sister's crazy about you.

I know.

She really is. I mean she's always worried about, "What's R. C. doing? What can we do for him?" and all of that. She's nuts about you.

Well, maybe she's afraid for me. "What's R. C. doing?" may actually mean, "What in the world does he think he's doing?" One of the great things about coming home is that I get to be with her as well. And when you all come up together to visit us in Virginia, that's a great thing too. It's hard for me when I tell my children, "Okay, we're going to go see . . . ," and I have to go through everybody instead of just "your grandparents." But it's the family coming together, and that's a wonderful thing.

Well, R. C., I'm just a little excited that you're here and that we're going to have this series on the family because I would like to have other people benefit the way I have from what you've learned. What you're talking about is not abstract theory. This thing has real shoe leather to it. You're walking the walk, not just talking the talk; so I'm looking forward with joyful anticipation to this series, and I want to thank you for coming to do it.

My pleasure.

1

THE FAMILY PLAN

My father and I have several things in common. One is that we are often asked difficult questions. The question he is asked more than any other is, "Where did evil come from?" The question I am asked more than any other is, "What's it like to have R. C. Sproul as your father?" His difficulty is theological; mine is conjectural. That is, I don't know how to answer my question because I have nothing with which to compare it. It's not as though I spent fifteen years as Michael Jordan's son, and now I'm R. C. Sproul's son.

I can tell you, however, two aspects of being his son that are probably unusual. Many times when I meet young men, I face the challenge of the gunslinger. They know they will probably never have a theological shoot-out with my father, so they settle for me. They delight to try to stump me, though when they succeed, the victory can be rather hollow. After all, it's not like they gunned down the real R. C. Sproul. Women, on the other hand, don't want to shoot me—they want to comfort me. They tend to be sensitive to the slings and arrows that come with being the son of . . .

There is also, to borrow a phrase, a *tertium quid*, a third option. Sometimes people meet me, get this puzzled look on their face, and note, "You sure don't look like your father." Then I point out where the family resemblance lies, in our mutual magnificent middles. We both have bellies to beat the band. There are a host of other similarities as well. We both write books. We both, from time to time, are on the radio. We have both served as pastors of churches. We are both Presbyterians. Oh, and we share a name as well.

Both of us likewise have great wives. I have outstanding children, while my poor father has only one, my sister. We do in some sense a similar kind of work, in the same way that a paper airplane and the Space Shuttle do similar kinds of things. We also believe essentially the same things. What you get with me, then, is an approximation of what he thinks, but lacking his depth of wisdom and skill of delivery.

There are, however, some significant differences between us as well. We come from different worlds. My father remembers World War II. I barely remember the soldiers coming home from Viet Nam. My father went through his teens when everyone liked Ike. When I was that age Ronald Reagan occupied the White House. And for all our similarities, I'm sure the bean counters at Visa are able to tell us apart. He, I'm sure, gets rather more leeway in his credit than I'll ever get.

But there is an important difference as well in the way we were raised. Yes, we both grew up in western Pennsylvania. But my father, when he grew up, lived not only with his mother, his father, and his sister, but an uncle, an aunt, a cousin, still more relations, and someone who wasn't even blood-related. When I was a boy there was just my mother, my father, and my sister. In my own house now, as I have grown, there are probably more people than there were in his house, but they still are only my immediate family. We have no aunts or uncles, though we have been blessed with six children, so far.

Not only, however, was there extended family in my father's home when he grew up, but the rest of the extended family was nearby. The Sprouls occupied several of the hills around Pittsburgh and often gathered the whole clan together to feast. I live amidst the hills of western Virginia, and my parents are over seven hundred miles away. My children's cousins are likewise hours and hours away by car. While there may be reasons for this separation, it remains a sad thing. We lack a closeness as families, at least geographically.

What caused this shift in family living arrangements? There is a battle, a critical front on the broader culture war, over the nature of the family. One of the weapons you need to fight a culture war is words. You want to have the good words on your side, if at all possible, and *family* is one of the best words. Everybody, after all, is in favor of families. If you can associate your agenda with "family," you will make headway in selling that agenda. Thus we have political campaigns being won or lost based on who succeeds in being perceived as for "family values." Now what are family values? The only thing I know about that has precious little to do with politics. I am a proponent of pro-family values because with six children, when I go to the grocery store I don't buy the large box, I don't buy the jumbo box, I buy the family-sized box of laundry detergent. I don't suppose that any political party, however, wants to be known as those who are in favor of big boxes of detergent. Even those who might have a tough row to hoe to claim the family values mantle have found a way to seize the word. You may have seen the bumper sticker that says, "Hate is not a family value." So those on the left latch onto "family" while pinning "hate," one of the bad words, on those on the right.

So a great battle is being waged over how we *define* the

family, and that is directly related to the battle for the *survival* of the family. Why would the enemies of God be intent on destroying the family? Because the family is one of precious few institutions established by God. The devil wants to destroy the family because the family matters. The sad news is that as the church joins this battle, we have joined it so late, and we're so far behind that we are fighting what strategists call a rearguard action. We're retreating while trying to save what we can. The typical vision of the family in the church, in fact, is so anemic that we think we're doing well if we can keep a husband and wife together while they raise a child or two. We think if we succeed in doing this, we ought to win a trophy. Only a generation or two ago, however, such a family would be looked upon with sadness as an almost family, as a portion of a family. Back then when people thought of family, they thought of homes like the one in which my father was raised. A generation ago when people thought of families they thought in terms of patriarchs and matriarchs. They had a multigenerational view, whereas now we're doing all we can simply to save the nuclear family.

Worse still, even when our families manage to stay together, we manage to tear them apart. The culture is content to let a husband, a wife, and one or two children share a roof, as long as it can ensure that they do not share a life. There need not be a divorce, a broken home to tear asunder a family. It happens within our homes. Popular culture looks at our families not as families but as a collection of individuals in disjointed demographic groups. Often even the designs of our homes reflect that shift in thinking. Too many homes are nothing more than apartment complexes, wherein each member of the "family" is given his or her own little space, complete with his or her own bathroom, his or her own television, his or her own Xbox. If we ever get together it's usually at the mess hall, and that is getting rarer every year. But even when we are all together under the same roof, we are still divided. Each demographic group has its own diversions to fill the time. Dad may have his nose buried in *Sports Illustrated*, while Mom is reading *Redbook*, or worse still, *Cosmopolitan*. Up in her room Princess is reading *Seventeen* magazine, while Junior is sitting in front of the television flipping through *Ranger Rick* magazine (if he reads anything at all). We may think, if we don't look beneath the surface, *What a lovely family.* But the truth is, this is a family already separated. If we could even get them together in one room, it would only be to watch the blue-eyed glowing idol in their living room.

But it gets worse: This isn't only true of society at large. We have much the same problem in the church. About the only time a typical family is all together when it comes to time at church is when they are riding there together in the car. We have a plethora of programs, all age- and often gender-segregated. Mom goes off to her Women in the Church or Awana circle. Dad heads off to his Promise Keepers meeting. Princess is at her youth group meeting, while Junior is watching videos of vegetables in children's church. We enter the house of God together, only to scatter in different directions. Even in the church we're being torn apart. We learned this, as we so often do, from the culture around us.

The rest of the week follows the same pattern. Come Monday Mom is off to her work, Dad is off to his, Princess is at the junior high school, and Junior is at the grade school. Everything about our modern culture pushes us away from each other. Each demographic group has its own language, its own musical styles, and on and on. Go to the mall, what I call the temple of consumption. There you will find as many as a half a dozen different sections of women's clothes, for half a dozen different ages. The generation gap no longer exists simply between teenagers and their parents, but between teenagers and tweenagers, and between tweenagers and twenty-somethings, *ad nauseam.*

We seem to think that if we can keep all this separateness together under one roof we are doing okay. But the truth is, we are failing miserably, even when we think we are succeeding. We're allowing our families to be torn apart because we are allowing our families to be molded by the wisdom of this world.

God, in His mercy and His power, has established in this world four institutions. One is the individual. The second is the family. After that comes the church. And finally He has also established the state. The drive in our age is to reduce that number down to two, to eliminate what the sociologists call the "mediating institutions," the family and the church. The culture looks at each of us principally as individuals who are likewise a part of the state. Our identity in the family or the church is seen as coincidental, if not problematic. But in actuality the family and the church are mediating or middle institutions, in that they protect us from being swallowed into one of the other two institutions. In this battle the world encourages us to think of our loyalties only in terms of ourselves as individuals or to the state. If a third loyalty is permitted, it is merely to our own demographic group. We then tend to think of ourselves by ourselves. We then lack a family identity. We then have no notion of being part of something bigger than ourselves. We are thus individualists rather than family-ists.

How do we fight this? What we find as we come to the

Word of God for our answers is this: We are kept together, we are bound together, we are a unity as families and as the church of Jesus Christ by and through the biblical understanding of the covenant. *Covenant* is one of those words and concepts that pop up over and over again in the Bible. It is central to our convictions, and it ought to be central to how we understand the Bible. But it also is central to our understanding of the family.

The relationship between the covenant and the family really hit home with me on a rather odd occasion. It happened when I was ordained to the ministry. In most Presbyterian denominations, the process of becoming a minister of the Gospel is something of an ordeal. We call this, in fact, our ordination trials. First you have to preach a sermon to a group of pastors and lay leaders in the denomination. Then you have to take an exam. But when all that is done, you have to "stand on the floor of the presbytery." That means those same men who listened to you preach with a watchful ear now are free to ask you questions. They can ask personal questions or theological questions, biblical questions or historical questions. My job, standing alone in front of all these godly men, is to answer the questions. Their goal in asking the questions is at least twofold. First, they want to make sure I know my stuff. Second, they want to make sure I don't believe anything completely off-the-wall. Also, I think, they want to see how eager I am to be ordained, if I'm willing to suffer through this ordeal.

Sometimes they'll ask you something easy like, "Tell us about how you came to know the Lord." Other times they'll ask for an outline of the book of Zephaniah. Or they might ask, "Please tell us a little about the great chain of salvation in Romans chapter 8." (Or they might fail to remind you that it's found in Romans 8.) During my trials I was asked this question: "Would you please list for us, Mr. Sproul, the covenants that God made with man?" "Yes," I started, because you'd better always start with "yes." "God made covenant with Adam. Then there was His covenant with Noah. Next was the Abrahamic covenant. He made covenant with David, and with Jesus."

The room in which I stood was not filled exclusively with godly men. At least one godly woman was also there, my own dear wife. After the whole ordeal was over, as we were driving back home, she told me that as I was answering the question on the covenants, one gentleman leaned over to another and said, "He forgot the covenant with Abraham." I said, "Isn't that interesting? Either that gentleman didn't hear me say 'the Abrahamic covenant' or he didn't know that 'Abrahamic' is the adjectival form meaning, 'of or pertaining to Abraham.'" But as we were having this conversation, a thought entered my mind. "You know, dear," I went on, "there actually was no covenant in the Bible with Abraham." She, of course, must have thought that my ordeal had caused me to flip my lid. "There was in fact," I went on, "no covenant with Adam, nor one with Noah, nor one with David. You see, every time God makes a covenant in the Bible, He always makes it 'with you *and your seed.*'"

God makes covenants with families, and in so doing, He binds us together. Covenants, in fact, are what define us as families. We are, as families, a group of people in covenant with God. We are unified by and for His covenant. But there is yet another level to the covenant and the family. Not only are we in covenant with God, we are likewise in covenant with each other. That is how I define the family—a series of horizontal covenants among men that is, as a whole, in vertical covenant with God. The horizontal covenants include, of course, the covenant between a husband and a wife, the covenant between a wife and a husband (this is what we are doing when making marriage vows—covenanting together), and the covenant between parents and children.

We haven't made much headway in defining the family, however, if we don't yet know what a covenant is. We may have some idea, but just as with the family, too often our understanding of the covenant has been distorted by the wisdom of the world. We tend, for instance to think of *covenant* as a rather pious and archaic word for contract. Contracts we understand. We deal with them all the time. We have contracts with our employers, contracts with our cell phone company, and some of us even have contracts with our book publishers. And there is a connection between covenants and contracts. When you have a contract, two parties come together in an agreement. One party promises to do one thing; the other party promises to do another. Crossway Books, for instance, has promised to try to persuade people to buy this book and to pay me a percentage of each sale. I, on the other hand, have promised to create this book and to deliver it by a particular date (which, by the way, is approaching way too rapidly).

But there is yet another similarity. Contracts often have penalties as well. If, for instance, Crossway fails to publish this book, they might have to pay a penalty. If I fail to meet my deadline, I might have to pay a penalty. Covenants, likewise, include commitments by the parties involved to perform some act or other. And they likewise include sanctions for failure to meet the terms of the agreement. So in some sense covenants are very much like contracts.

The differences, however, are critical. Contracts are something over which there are negotiations. The two parties come to the negotiating table and see if they can hammer out an agreement. Suppose, for instance, Crossway had offered me all the brussels sprouts I could eat in exchange for this book. Would I have to take this deal? Of course not. Or suppose that I sent Crossway a manuscript that consisted of hundreds of pages of "Families are good" repeated over and over. Would they have an obligation to publish the book? By no means. Either party can walk away from the negotiations before there is agreement.

Understand that when God came to Abraham and said, "Abraham, have I got a deal for you! I am going to give you a son. I'm going to give you a land. I'm going to bring nations from you. I'm going to bless the nations through you. But wait, there's more—I also will be your God," Abraham was not free to reply, "That's a great opening offer, Lord. Throw in thirty wives and you have a deal." And God wouldn't counteroffer, "I'll give you ten wives, but you'll have to give up the land." There is no back and forth when God makes covenant with man. When God speaks, that settles the matter. Sadly, not only do we want to come into our families and negotiate, but we want to do the same with God. "God, I'll do this, and I'll do that. I'll obey this law and that law. But this other one, you know the one, we're going to have to have some serious talks about that."

In like manner, we allow the world to define what the family is, what the family is called to be. We think we can remake the family in any manner we wish. But the horizontal covenants are determined by the vertical covenant. *God* decides how things will work. Not only are the covenants with God not something we can negotiate over, they are also not something we can refuse. That is, God didn't say, "Here's the deal. You can take it or leave it." Rather He tells us, "Here's the deal." We can't escape the authority of God, no matter how much the world tells us we can. In fact, the very essence of the family covenant is that we cannot escape God's authority.

The verse in all the Old Testament that was most central to the heart of the children of Israel, the passage that defined them as a people and that we know as the *shema*, Deuteronomy 6:4, says: "Hear, O Israel: The LORD our God, the LORD is one." What follows that is the great commandment, "You shall love the LORD your God with all your heart and with all your soul and with all your might." What follows that? Over and over for the rest of this most sacred chapter God commands, "Tell your children, tell your children, tell your children. Tell them who I am. Tell them what I have done. Tell them what I require. Teach them My covenants."

My prayer is that through this book we might develop a more covenantal, a more biblical understanding of the family. I pray we will catch that ancient vision, that we will strive to keep covenant in our families, for our families, and as families. I pray that we will be equipped to put back together, by God's covenantal grace, what the world has torn asunder, the family. We can pray such with confidence, because we serve a God who is not only Lord of the covenant but is also our loving Father. And He never has and never will break covenant, no matter what the cost.

2

THE FAMILY'S CHIEF END

We noted in the last chapter that a great war is being fought in our culture over the nature of the family. Principalities and powers among us would delight to see us have a confused, distorted understanding of what the family is. If we belong to Christ, we know, however, that our understanding of the family needs to come not from the world, but from the Word of God. Only the Bible can tell us rightly what the family is.

Our tendency in the church, I'm afraid, is to mix together the Bible's understanding of the family with the world's understanding of the family. We perform too narrow a reformation in our thinking. When the world shows us Heather and her two mommies, we rightly react against it. But we fail to see clearly and fully what is wrong with this picture. If we want to understand the nature of the family in a biblical way, we need not only to understand what are its constituent parts, but what is its goal or purpose. In which direction, toward what end, are we to be leading our families? The best place to find that answer is to go back to the beginning, to find out where the family came from. To do that, we need to turn to Genesis 2.

Most of us are somewhat familiar with the content of Genesis 2. We know that there Moses records similar things to what he recorded in chapter 1 of Genesis. In both places, under the inspiration of the Holy Spirit, without error, Moses tells us how God created the world. He tells us what God did the first day, and the second, and so on. My children, when they took their very first history test, went to the beginning. We asked them, "What did God do on day one? What did God do on day two?" They passed with flying colors.

Because there is a battle over this portion of the Bible in the culture, because so many people refuse to believe God on the issue of creation, we too often tend to look at these chapters as mere fodder for the battle. And in so doing we miss some important themes. God did not inspire Moses to write these words principally so that two thousand years later we would know how to answer Darwinists. We often miss how He ended His day. We are told several times, "And God saw that it was good." God pronounces His divine benediction or His good word on His own creative work. He assesses what He has done and announces that He is pleased with His work. God is here speaking prophetically, pronouncing a state of weal upon the creation. No doubt, had we been there, we would have concurred.

Of course, for us there is a bit of dramatic irony going on. Though Moses has made no mention of it yet, we are well aware that there is in the background something rather sinister. We know the serpent is coming soon. So while we're hearing, "And it was good . . . and it was good . . . and it was good," in the background we hear some scary mood music. What's interesting, however, is that God doesn't wait until the serpent steps onto the scene to pronounce His first malediction. God declared that there was something not good long before the serpent first slithered onto the scene. Moses tells us in Genesis 2:18, "Then the LORD God said, 'It is not good that the man should be alone.'"

Our tendency with this passage is to stop right here. If we were to peruse all the books on the family purporting to be written from a Christian perspective, I suspect we would find that most, if not all, of them would come to this passage, just as I have done. That it is not good that man should be alone, and that God so decreed it, ought to let us know how important marriage and family are. And the passage does tell us that. But it tells us so much more.

We have to ask, "Why is it not good that man should be alone?" These same "Christian" books will posit their own theories. "Oh," they might say, "it is not good because men are from Mars and women are from Venus. God knew that they would need each other to balance each other one out." Or they might reason, "Poor Adam there in the garden all alone. What he needed was companionship. We are, after all, social creatures. So God made Eve to keep Adam company. Companionship is the point of the family, what marriage is all about." We agree with God. It is a problem that man is alone. But we leave God behind as we try to figure out what the problem is.

Adam, you will remember, has made no complaint. God didn't declare His divine displeasure after Adam came and whined that he was lonely. It wasn't his idea; he didn't say, "God, it is not good that I am alone." The answer as to why it is not good, the revelation of the problem, is found in the answer God gives in the rest of the passage: "Then the LORD God said, 'It is not good that the man should be alone; I will make a helper fit for him.'" The problem is clear enough— Adam doesn't need a soul-mate. He doesn't need a boon to his self-esteem. He doesn't need a balance. What Adam needed was help. He was incapable on his own.

I understand why I need help. I am reminded of my insufficiency daily. But why did Adam need help? Was it because the ground stubbornly refused to be fruitful? Of course not. Adam was in paradise. And he wasn't planning on leaving on a trip. God did not say, "Adam needs a helper because he's going to get lost. He won't, because he's a man, stop and ask for directions. I'll make him a woman to tell Adam how to find his way." You can't look at this picture of Adam in the garden and argue that something's missing here in paradise. If we want to know why Adam needs help, we need to go further back, into Genesis 1: "Then God said, 'Let us make man in our image, after our likeness. And let them have dominion over the fish of the sea and over the birds of the heavens and over the livestock and over all the earth and over every creeping thing that creeps on the earth.' So God created man in his own image, in the image of God he created him; male and female he created them. And God blessed them. And God said to them, 'Be fruitful and multiply and fill the earth and subdue it and have dominion over the fish of the sea and over the birds of the heavens and over every living thing that moves on the earth'" (Genesis 1:26-28). Here we find God's charge to Adam, God's covenant with Adam. It was not good that man should be alone as he set about the business of exercising dominion over the creation.

The creation or dominion mandate, of course, was given in the context of the garden. Adam and Eve yet are without sin. The ground would cooperate with their labors and bear much fruit. But then the serpent makes his appearance, and all the joy of the creation comes crashing down in the Fall. Adam and Eve are no longer what they once were. They are at enmity with God, separated from Him. Now they, and all who would flow from them, are spiritually dead. So now what does God have in store for them?

While Adam and Eve could, and did, change, God Himself does not and cannot change. And neither does the covenant. Neither does the dominion mandate. Consider the curses that God pronounces in the aftermath of the Fall. Adam is not fired from his job. He is not told, "You shall no longer rule over the creation." Instead he is told that the creation will be more stingy in its obedience. Eve is not told that she will no longer be fruitful and multiply. Rather she is told that now as she gives birth, there will be with it great pain. They are expelled from the garden, but the command abides.

The Scripture then gives us a brief overview of ancient history, tracing the line of Seth and the line of Cain side by side. Eventually the two sides become indistinguishable as the power of sin grows over the creation. God, in His just wrath, sends the Flood to wipe out every living thing, except for Noah, his wife, their sons, their wives, and all the animals on the ark. God in His grace dries up the water, and as Noah leaves the ark God speaks His law once more: "And God blessed Noah and his sons and said to them, 'Be fruitful and multiply and fill the earth'" (Genesis 9:1). It is the same command. The dominion mandate abides. It does not change.

It still hasn't changed to this day, except in one important way. When the original command was given, we were in paradise. Now not only do we have ground that wants to produce thorns and thistles, not only do we no longer have peace among the animals, not only does childbirth bring with it great pain, but the dominion mandate must now be done in the context of perpetual conflict. The job remains, but now instead of exercising dominion in a context of peace, with God's blessing, warfare surrounds us.

After Adam and Eve fall into sin, God comes to visit them in the garden. He asks why they are hiding, and they expose their sin by confessing their nakedness. God asks if they have eaten the fruit, and the blame game begins. Eve blames the serpent. Adam blames first Eve ("The woman . . . gave me the fruit of the tree") and then, in a backward kind of way, God Himself ("whom you gave to be with me"). We've looked briefly at God's curse on Adam and Eve and have seen that hope abides because they yet have their task before them. But the great news comes in the context of the curse upon the serpent: "The LORD God said to the serpent, 'Because you have done this, cursed are you above all livestock and above all beasts of the field; on your belly you shall go, and dust you shall eat all the days of your life. I will put enmity between you and the woman, and between your offspring and her offspring; he shall bruise your head, and you shall bruise his heel'" (Genesis 3:14-15). For this last part I prefer the New International Version, which says, "he will crush your head, and you will strike his heel." This, in any translation, is God's solemn declaration of war.

The devil had already been waging war. That's how the Fall happened. What he does in the garden is recruit not only Adam and Eve to join him in his rebellious army, but with them, all of their children. Before God even enters the garden, so to speak, the battle lines are already drawn. It's not as if God's approach elicits glee in the hearts of Adam and Eve, as they look for Him to punish the serpent. On one side of the battlefield stands God. On the other stands the devil, Adam, and Eve. But what is God's promise? He does not say to the serpent, "You know, my good friends Adam and Eve and I are going to get you before everything is said and done." Instead He promises, "I will put enmity between you and the woman, and between your offspring and her offspring."

The only way Adam and Eve can change sides in this battle is if God, in His grace, puts enmity in their hearts against the serpent. After the Fall, by nature we are friends—indeed children—of the serpent and are at enmity with God. Once the change has been made, Adam and Eve will not leave the battlefield but will now fight *for* rather than *against* their Maker. With the cryptic allusion to the bruising of the heel of the Seed of the Woman we are given, right after the fall into sin, the first hint of the Gospel. In fact, theologians call this promise the proto-gospel, the first gospel.

But it is more than that. This passage also marks what I call the proto-eschaton, the first hint of the end of all things. We are told not only that the serpent will bruise the heel of the Seed of the Woman, but that the serpent will likewise be bruised or crushed. We are told here for the first time that in the end Jesus wins, that His kingdom wins. When Jesus enters the scene, does He still tell us, "Be fruitful and multiply. Exercise dominion over every living thing"? Yes and no. The command of Jesus is this: "But seek first the kingdom of God and his righteousness, and all these things will be added to you" (Matthew 6:33). The exercising of dominion over all the created order is the same as making manifest the reign of the kingdom of God over all things. That's what Adam was made for. That's what Eve was made for, to help Adam in this task. And, not surprisingly, that's what the Bride of Christ, the Second Adam, was made to do, to be a help to the New Adam as He fulfills His calling. The Bible, friends, is one book, and that one book is a family portrait.

We miss this, once again, because we have drunk so deeply

from the wells of the world. The world has its own peculiar
goal. Everyone wants their marriages to be enriching, fulfilling, and exciting. And everyone wants their children to grow
up to be prosperous. The world is in a mad dash in pursuit
of personal peace and affluence. Sadly, too often in the evangelical church it is not much different. Of course we want our
children to become Christians. But too often that is just an
addition to the all-consuming goal that they would attain
their own personal peace and affluence. We pray that they
will be Christians just like us, who have found their way in
the world. But the command of God for us and our children
is not that we would find our way in the world, but that we
would wage war with the world.

Isn't this just like us, and isn't this just like God? He has
given us a task, a charge, a mandate. He has designed us
specifically for the serving of this purpose. Families are made
for this warfare. But like Adam and Eve before us, we have
our own plans. We go in search of some other job to do. We
seek out some other source for meaning, for significance in
our lives. That's how we get so confused over the family. This
is how we come to believe that the family exists for us, that
we find in each other our self-esteem, that we might find
mutual love and admiration. Of course, self-esteem rightly
understood (a rare thing indeed) is appropriate. I hope our
marriages are marked by mutual love and admiration. But
this is not what they are for. That's not why the family exists.
We do not exist for happiness.

We're confused because while the world offers its tempta-
tions—"Don't get married, so you can enjoy your freedom
and joy the rest of your life"—we in the church again reform
only slightly. We don't teach that we need to die to self, but
rather suggest that a good Christian marriage is the only way

to get that self-interested freedom, that self-referential joy. We argue that the problem with the world isn't that people serve the self, but that they serve the self poorly. To serve the self well requires the church. We offer marriage seminars promising that we know the key to greater joy, to greater intimacy, to greater excitement. While it may be true that monogamy is the ultimate aphrodisiac, only a fool would marry for that reason.

Earlier in this chapter I made a little quip at the expense of John Gray. He became famous with the publication of his book *Men Are from Mars, Women Are from Venus*. I've never read the book, and I probably never will. But I think I understand the basic premise, and I actually think there might be something to it. I think so because I am a man, and I am from Mars. No, though I am little, I am not green. Rather I mean that I see my life in terms of challenge, quest, warfare, and adventure. That's what men do. This reflects the outward call of the dominion task. Men go into the jungle and turn it into a garden. Men are by nature conquerors, which is why it makes such perfect sense that Jesus calls us to this task. In Him we are more than conquerors. The difference is that we do this for Him rather than for ourselves. Dominion is all about conquest; that's what we're made for. Men live for a cause, and this is the cause, the crusade to which we have been called—to make manifest the reign of Jesus Christ.

Could there be a more glorious crusade? Would you rather conquer Europe like Napoleon? To conquer the known world like Alexander the Great? To conquer the universe like Han Solo? To win the heavyweight championship of the world like Rocky Balboa? None of that amounts to a hill of beans. The cause I'm involved in, and the cause my family is involved in, is world conquest and dominion over all things for the glory of Jesus Christ. This alone can satisfy a man.

But what about our wives? John Gray hits on the truth there as well. Women long for intimacy. That's the way they are made. What, though, could be more intimate, more romantic, more dramatic than a shared vision as grand as making visible the invisible reign of Jesus Christ? My dear wife and I have, so far, six little warriors. That's a lot of diapers. Do you think that my wife and I could work our way through this mountain of diapers simply by gritting our teeth and saying, "Well, I suppose this is what God wants us to do"? No, we do this because we understand that changing diapers is an integral part of the quest, part of the cause. Together my wife and I are building the kingdom of God, exercising dominion, beating back the weeds of stinky diapers, tending the garden God has put us in. This is why my dear wife vacuums the floor, for it is a part of the garden she has been called to dress and to keep. But she is doing this not as raw duty, but because she understands that she is exercising dominion over the dust for the glory of Christ. Can you beat that for intimacy or sharing in a cause together? Can you beat that for romance? This is what covenant families are called to do. This is what we are made for. And there is nothing more grand, nothing more glorious, nothing more exciting, nothing more consuming, nothing more binding.

It binds us also with our children. While I am raising my children to be soldiers in this great war, I am not raising them so that someday they can be soldiers. Rather, even *now* we fight side by side. They do not wait until they are on their own to be about the Lord's business. They are engaged in warfare right now. Every time my children walk together with me through the grocery store, every time they remember to say,

"Thank you, ma'am" to the lady behind the counter who gives them a cookie, they are making manifest the reign of Christ. It is not something for later, but something we share in now. Together, as a family, bound together, we pursue the glory of God through making known the glory of His Son.

God, as always, spoke wisely when He told us it is not good that man should be alone. And He showed forth His grace in binding us together in and as families. May He continue, in His grace, to raise up faithful families, families that recognize and are obedient to their calling. May He fill His church with families filled with a single passion: to seek first the Kingdom of His dear Son.

3

THE COVENANT HUSBAND

From time to time it is my pleasure to go to different towns to speak at different churches and at various conferences. There are certain ceremonies or liturgies that tend to go almost unnoticed at conferences, unless you go to as many as I do. Before you get up to speak, you first must listen as some poor soul goes through the difficult task of introducing you. The idea is to tell those assembled that it would be a good and prudent thing for them to listen to what is about to be said, not because the organizers went to great trouble and expense to get me there, but because I'm supposed to be deemed a fairly reliable guy. Now when the whole thing is being set up, those who are good planners and know this part of the liturgy is coming will ask, "Do you have a bio you can send us?" I do have a bio. It's a page of tiny print that lists just about everything I've ever done that doesn't cause me great shame. The introducer's job is to pick those parts he deems most relevant for his task.

Each time this happens I go through an internal struggle. Sometimes that struggle leads to a rebuke to my introducer. Most of the time he will speak of my work on this magazine or that or mention that I wrote a book on this theme and edited another on some other theme. Then I come forward. I typically explain that while what the introducer said was true, what was missed was the center of what I am. If the goal is to introduce R. C. Sproul, Jr., or even if the goal were to list my greatest accomplishments, it would go something like this: "R. C. is the husband of Denise and the father of Darby, Campbell, Shannon, Delaney, Erin Claire, and Maili." That is both what I do and what I am. I need to remember that, for this is about my calling from God as a husband and a father. My identity must be determined not by well-meaning friends, not by the world around me, but by God, my Maker.

Those in the world have their own system for determining who I am. They have me pegged in a particular demographic group. I'm lumped in with other lumpy men and so receive e-mails for weight loss pills and programs. I receive flyers in the mail for products guaranteed to stop male pattern baldness. Once or twice a year I even receive a catalog of products designed specifically for the Pittsburgh Steelers fan. And one day, in the not too distant future, the folks at AARP will have their sights on me. While I may be tempted to understand myself in light of these groups, I'm called to do otherwise. These things are not my identity at all. I have taken on a different name. Because my identity connects with a 2,000-year-old Jewish carpenter, it is connected with all others who have the same identity. And Christ has called me to live out that identity as a husband and as a father. To understand that, we have to go to the Bible, back once again to the dominion mandate. God has, as with Adam, given me a helper in my dear wife. But as with Adam, having that helper doesn't undo the charge. I am a son of Adam, and so I am yet called to exercise dominion over the creation.

It is usually not a difficult sell to get husbands and fathers to see their calling in light of the dominion mandate. It isn't a long theoretical walk from dressing and keeping a garden to the work that we do in the world. Nor is it a stretch to see that even if we are not farmers, we still face thorns and thistles in our work. As a magazine editor I have to deal with printers who don't keep their promises and angry readers who are content to have their existing convictions confirmed but don't want them challenged. When I am able to be a part of a team that can bring together wood turned into paper and thinking turned into teaching, then I am exercising dominion. The dominion mandate relates to my work, but not only to my work. There is more to it.

In the evangelical church, at least as compared to the world around us, we are fairly traditional. As the culture moves away from the biblical ideal of the family, our vision on how to deal with this tends to move back to another cultural idea that is slightly better. We recognize that our family ought not to be modeled after the hapless Simpsons on television. We think it far better to model our families in the image of Mr. Cleaver, Beaver's daddy, not realizing that the one is the father of the other (that is, the culture wrought by one vision of the family gave birth to our current culture). Too often we come to the issue of the father's role as traditionalists, as conservatives, believing that the man's job is to go out and bring home the bacon. Of course, we are a little accommodating to the world around us, agreeing that after we get home from work, it would be a good thing to help out with the supper dishes from time to time. We think the man is called to make the money, or the bulk thereof, to help the wife a bit with her work, and, at least in the summertime, to cook the meat outside. If we can get that done, then we've done our job.

This *is* a part of our job. Adam did bring home the bacon, in the bread he sweated out of the ground. We ought to do the same. But this is not the center of our calling. For we who are husbands and fathers, the center of our calling is not to exercise dominion out in the jungle where we make our living, but in our homes. My job in life isn't to write books or to speak at conferences. Instead my job focuses on my wife and my children. I cannot, like Samuel or Eli or even David, pat myself on the back for a job well done when I fail to do well by my wife and children. Our families are not some separate slice of our lives. Instead they are the very center of our calling in exercising dominion and in seeking the kingdom.

I'm afraid we miss this because we're sissies. We know, despite the thorns and thistles, that coaxing a living out of the ground is comparatively easy. Every man out there is willing to say, "Okay, I'll be a traditional, conservative father. I can do that. But, dear wife, you do the family thing. You take care of that. I'll hug and kiss the kids when I get home from work, if they're still awake, but you take care of the rest." But this is not our calling.

We will look at the calling of the husband, at the calling of the wife, and at the calling of the children. We will see, I pray, how profoundly interrelated these roles are, and at the important distinctions among them. But first, if we are ever going to have families that honor and obey God, we have to master this point, that as husbands and fathers our central task, our central garden that we are called to dress and till, is our family. Which means this: When you wake up every morning, you need to ask yourself these questions: "What can I do today to manifest the kingdom of Christ? What can I do today to exercise dominion in and through my family?"

This is essentially what Paul was getting at when he addressed the men in the church at Ephesus. There he gives us a picture of what it means to be a husband. "Husbands, love your wives, as Christ loved the church and gave himself up for her" (Ephesians 5:25). This is Paul's command, given under the unerring inspiration of the Holy Spirit. I've known husbands who used this difficult call as a palliative in getting their wives to swallow Paul's command to the wife. "Dear," they say, "I know it must be a difficult calling to submit to me. But can't you see that my own calling is difficult as well, that I'm supposed to love you as Christ loved the church and gave Himself for her?" The next step is to make the claim that we actually have fulfilled this calling, at least hypothetically speaking. We reason with our wives this way: "Suppose that I someday take you for a vacation to New York City. Now if I took you to New York City, perhaps I might get us a room at the Waldorf-Astoria. And if that happened, it just might happen that I would take you to see a Broadway play. Then suppose, just for the sake of this argument, that I would take you to the Four Seasons for supper. After we finished, if I were to do all this, then we would go for a walk in Central Park. We might walk hand in hand, and naturally I would fail to notice the sun going down. After all, I'm so struck by your beauty that I don't even know if the stars are out tonight. I can't tell if it's cloudy or bright. I only have eyes for you. Now if all this were to happen, and if, as we walked along, a mugger should emerge from behind a bush, holding a gun and demanding, 'Your money or your life,' if all this were to happen, then I know with confidence that I would step between you and the mugger, shielding you so that you might escape. I would take that bullet and die for you if that should ever happen. Therefore, because I would give up my life in this hypothetical situation, I love you as Christ loved the church and gave Himself for her."

Is this what Paul meant when he drew the comparison between the church and Christ and the wife and husband? To ask perhaps a more difficult, and earlier, question, which part of this analogy came first? Did God institute marriage in order to reflect the reality of the relationship of Christ and His church, or did He simply use the nearly universal experience of marriage as a handy tool to explain the relationship of Christ and the church? As is so often the case, the answer is both. Marriage was designed to be a picture of Christ and His bride precisely because they both intersect in the issue of exercising dominion. Eve was given to Adam that he might fulfill the dominion mandate. And the church is given to Jesus, the second Adam, that He might fulfill the dominion mandate, that all things might be brought under subjection.

Just as Adam's focus, however, is on his bride, so too is the focus of Jesus upon His bride. We see that, and we avoid the silly reduction of the husband's call to taking a hypothetical bullet if we simply continue to read what Paul has to say: He "gave himself up for her, that he might sanctify her, having cleansed her with the washing of water with the word, so that he might present the church to himself in splendor, without spot or wrinkle or any such thing, that she might be holy and without blemish."

We miss this because we miss the work of Christ. We think that when Jesus cried out in triumph on the cross, "It is finished," all of His work was finished. We think Jesus is merely sitting up in heaven waiting for time to end, that He is not busy about the work His Father gave Him to do. He finished paying for our sins, allowing the Father to judge us as righteous. But Christ is still about the business of sanctifying His bride. This, and not taking the potential bullet, is the frightening calling upon husbands. Our job is to sanctify our wives and by extension our own children. This is a harder job than making a living, a harder job than taking a bullet. It is a lifelong, uninterrupted job, that of being a tool in the sanctification of our wives and children. How can we possibly do it?

We do it, I believe, by exercising the roles Christ exercises for the church for our families. John Calvin spoke of Jesus fulfilling the *munis triplex*, the threefold role. The Westminster Shorter Catechism says, in answer to the question, "What offices does Christ execute as our redeemer?": "Christ as our redeemer executes the offices of a prophet, of a priest and of a king, both in His estate of humiliation and exaltation." If we would be Christ to our wives and children, this is likewise our calling.

What, though, is a *prophet*? Our tendency is to think of the prophet simply in terms of foretelling the future, as if the prophet is a godly form of the fortune-teller. It is certainly true that from time to time God revealed to His prophets things that were to come. This, however, is not the center of what it means to be a prophet, either in the Bible or in our homes. The function of the prophet instead was to bring the Word of God to bear on His people. One way of describing the work of a prophet is that he serves as God's lawyer, which brings us back to the covenant. God sends the prophet to bring suit against His people for violating the terms of His covenant. The prophet says, "Thus saith the Lord, 'You have failed to keep My covenant. I told you to do this and not to do that, but you have done what you were not to do, and have not done what you were to do.'" God then calls the mountains, the trees, and the people as His witnesses, who likewise profess that the people have broken covenant.

This too is what husbands are to do. We are to wash our wives with the Word, to bring to bear the Word of God in the lives of our families. When we remind our wives not to have a complaining spirit but to rejoice in all things, we are fulfilling our prophetic role. When we remind our children as they wrestle over who will be first in some game that the first will be last and the last will be first, we are again seeking to wash away the spots and stains, to purify, to beautify the garden that is our family. We are not just cleansing our families but are doing so with the very Word of God. We cleanse from our families those thoughts, words, and deeds that do not match up with what the Word of God commands.

This job requires some of the sacrifice that Christ shows for us. The reality is that when our wives or our children are caught up in a particular sin, when they have a spot or a wrinkle, the last thing they want from us is to be reminded of it. They want to be left alone in their sin, because just like husbands and fathers, they are sinners. Nobody likes having their spots shown up, do they? Which means that as we fulfill our prophetic role, we should not be surprised that our wives and children get mad at us. This is not a pleasant thing for a husband and father. We like to be liked. But we are not called to be liked. We are called to be faithful. The work of the prophet is almost always lonely work, and not appreciated.

The prophet's mantel, however, is not all we are called to pick up. The second role we take as Christ to our family, as fathers and husbands, is the role of *the priest*. We need to be careful here. This is where to some degree the analogy breaks down. Husbands are like Christ, and wives like the church, but there is not a one-to-one correspondence. We are called to be Christlike, but we cannot do all that Christ did. We cannot, and it would be blasphemy to even try to, atone for the sins of our family. Christ as our priest is also our substitute. He not only *makes* sacrifice for us but *is* our sacrifice. Husbands, though they must live sacrificial lives, do not atone for their families.

But there is more to the priestly role than the making of sacrifice. The prophet is one who brings the Word of God to His people. The priest is one who brings the word of the people to God. As fathers and husbands, we must bring our families daily before the throne of God, before His mercy seat. We are, as Moses did for the children of Israel, to plead with God on behalf of our families. When I put my children to bed each night, like most Christian parents, I pray with and for my children. Every night I ask, "Lord, please bless these children." Now, what do I mean by "bless"? Am I asking God to let the children find a winning lottery ticket along the side of the road? Of course not. The blessing I seek for my children is that they will grow in grace, that they will show forth in greater and greater abundance the fruit of His Spirit. I pray that He will make my children great and mighty warriors in the great battle to which He has called all of us.

I am, rather like Job who made sacrifices for his children, coming before the Lord for them. When we still had only a few children, even the posture of our praying communicated the priestly role of the father. At the conclusion of our nightly family worship I would take the children into my lap, put my arms around them, and place my hands on their heads. In so doing I was communicating to the children, "I am your covenant head. I am your God-ordained protection and shield. As your priest I will bring you before the presence of our Lord."

Husbands, this does not apply only to our children. I would venture to guess there is nothing your wife wants more from you than that you should do the same for her, that you would pray with and for your wife. Wives crave intimacy, and nothing is more intimate than coming together before our King in prayer. This is better than buying flowers, greater than remembering to pick up your towel, more powerful than diamonds and pearls. Nothing will communicate more clearly your love for your wife than her hearing you beseech the God of heaven and earth for her. If we would be a prophet, we must also be a priest, interceding for our families, even as our Lord intercedes for us.

Being a *king*, we men figure, is a piece of cake. It's good to be the king. But we have to remember for what purpose we have been made the king in our home. A king is the covenant head over the kingdom, which is far more about responsibility than it is about privilege.

In our ten years of marriage my dear wife and I have been on three different cruises. We like to cruise, at least when we're not on the cruise. Usually, once we board we wonder why we're there. Cruise ships are technological marvels. Many of the commercial cruise ships carry over two thousand guests and over a thousand staff. That's bigger than my hometown, by a factor of fourteen. They are essentially cities that float. Each ship that we traveled on had one big dining room. There were two sittings of a thousand passengers each.

Overseeing this city is the captain of the ship. He serves as the king. The reason, in fact, that ships' captains are authorized to perform wedding ceremonies is connected to this idea. In the open seas there are no laws, no governments. The captain, then, is the sovereign on the sea and so can perform weddings. But with that high privilege comes enormous responsibility. When I sit down to eat in that dining room, if my spoon is greasy, responsibility for it falls on the busboy, on the headwaiter, on the maitre d', on the head of the dining room, and fully and finally on the captain of the ship. He, because he is head over everything, answers for everything. So it is for the husband and father.

Every spot, every wrinkle on the wife and children, is the king's responsibility. I know this is scary, a weight we don't want. But the king is called to face up to the frightening things. That it is overwhelming or threatening doesn't change that it is real. You cannot escape your responsibilities as a husband and father simply because they scare you. You can't quit. But it is also important for husbands to remember that we too are the bride. That is, as the church, we have a Husband in Christ. He has promised to cleanse us, to purify us. He is where we find the strength to fulfill the very call He gives us as husbands. Unlike us, this Husband has all power. Unlike us, this Husband is perfectly righteous. Unlike us, this Husband has infinite grace to shower upon us. The answer to the fear is not to cower in our bunker but to pray for courage. May our King stiffen our resolve, expand our vision, and equip us unto every good work.

4

THE COVENANT WIFE

Years ago one of my responsibilities in working with my
father was to help plan the content of his radio program, *Renewing Your Mind*. I didn't tell him what to say,
mind you. I simply made suggestions of things it would be
good for him to talk about. He, of course, is capable of
teaching well on a variety of subjects. We did series on particular books of the Bible, historical series, theological series,
even philosophical series. But among my favorites and, based
on the response from listeners, among their favorites were
programs built on what we call "The Hard Sayings." We did
a week or so of shows on "Hard Sayings of the Old
Testament," another on "Hard Sayings of Jesus," another on
"Hard Sayings of the Prophets."

A "saying" is qualified to be considered hard in a few
ways. First were those hard sayings that were difficult to
understand. What does Peter possibly mean when he tells us
that Jesus preached to the spirits in prison (1 Peter 3:19)? But
second were those passages that were easy to understand but
hard to swallow. When God destroys Nadab and Abihu for
offering strange fire in His presence, we understand what
happened, but are still shocked by it. In like manner, in this

chapter we will deal with a passage that is abundantly clear but extremely difficult to swallow. It is the passage that I call the "Yes, but . . ." passage, because as evangelicals we have to say yes to it, but we want to kill it with a thousand qualifications. The passage is Ephesians 5, verses 22 through 24: "Wives, submit to your own husbands, as to the Lord. For the husband is the head of the wife even as Christ is the head of the church, his body, and is himself its Savior. Now as the church submits to Christ, so also wives should submit in everything to their husbands."

We can't, no matter how we'd like to, escape the plain meaning of Paul's injunction here. Nor can we, if we want to hold onto the authority of the Bible, dismiss this simply as Paul's injunction. These are God's words. That's why we have to say yes. We must concede that God calls wives to submit to their own husbands, but we are told it doesn't mean this or it doesn't mean that, until finally we are left with wives doing whatever they want.

There is, however, at least one qualification that does not fall into the category of attempts to wiggle out from under the command of God. How are wives to submit to their husbands? "As to the Lord." In case you're not clear on this, Paul makes it terribly clear for us. The submission that is called for here isn't merely submission that the church actually demonstrates to Christ, but the genuine submission we are commanded to offer to Christ.

We have difficulty with this in large part because we live in an individualistic age. The world around us is steeped in egalitarianism. Egalitarianism is a fancy way of saying equalitarianism. This philosophy affirms, as our Constitution does, that all men are created equal, but it fails to include appropriate qualifiers as to the nature of that equality. It affirms not only that all people are equal before the law, not only that all people are equal in dignity and value, not only that all people are made in the image of God, but that all people are equal in authority, in relationships, and with respect to roles. This drives us to add the "buts" to Paul, but it comes from a failure to distinguish between role and ontology.

Ontology, I know, is not a word we use every day. It is part of the language of philosophers. It means of or pertaining to being. We get confused on submission because we, at least in this context, can't see a distinction between role and the thing in itself. Because of this confusion, we think that when God calls wives to submit to their husbands, this is the same as God saying that women are less than men. We think submission equals less value, less dignity, less being made in the image of God. Our solution to this confusion, too often, is to deny the plain teaching of Scripture. We don't want the Bible to teach that women are less valuable or less important than men (which is a good thing, because the Bible doesn't teach that), but we think it says such here in Ephesians, and so we try to escape it. We try to undo what Paul is saying.

The better solution is to go once again back to the beginning, to how God created man. It was God Himself who said, "It is not good that the man should be alone; I will make him a helper fit for him" (Genesis 2:18). Some translations say, in an older style of English, a helper "meet" to him. "Meet" means fitting or appropriate. What you see in this language is the very point I'm belaboring. There is at the same time an equality and a distinction. Eve is made to be a helper to Adam. This affirms that she is in a position of submission. (This is made all the more clear when Adam names his wife, as naming was a sign of authority.)

But at the same time we are told that this helper is com-

parable to him. This speaks to the other side of the equa-
tion—her value, her dignity, her worth; in this way she is
equal to Adam. Like Adam she is made in the image of God.
Thus it makes sense that God would say, "In the image of
God he created him; male and female he created them"
(Genesis 1:27).

If this isn't sufficient to put to rest the egalitarian error,
there is only one place left to go. We've gone all the way back
to the beginning, but now we have to go back before the
beginning. We have to go back to the very first covenant. This
covenant, however, is not the dominion mandate. Rather it is
a covenant made among the members of the Trinity, what
theologians call the covenant of redemption. I venture to
guess that if we were to poll professing Christians about the
covenant of redemption, most if not all of them would suggest that this is God's covenant with man, whereby our sins
are atoned for by Christ at Calvary and His righteousness
becomes ours by faith. They would think we were talking
about how we have peace with God. Technically speaking,
however, the covenant of redemption isn't how we have
peace with God. It is not even a covenant between God and
man. Instead the first covenant was made among the members of the Trinity.

We affirm that in His counsels before all time the Father
spoke to the Son something like this: "This is the plan—this
is what We're going to do. I'm going to elect a people for You,
a bride. Son, You're going to take on flesh, and You're going
to tabernacle among them. You will obey all of My revealed
will, keeping My law. But You will receive the wrath due to
the sons of disobedience. I will curse You and forsake You,
so that those whom I have chosen will have their sins covered.
Your righteousness will be deemed their righteousness." The

Father then explained to the Spirit His role, that He would give life where there was only death, to those who were chosen, that He would indwell those whom He had quickened, and that He would lead these same to greater and greater obedience, to reflect more and more the character of Christ.

Who is giving the orders here? In the covenant of redemption it is clearly God the Father. The Son is in a subordinate role to the Father. It seems that in John's Gospel, every time you turn around Jesus is saying, "I'm doing My Father's will," "I'm speaking My Father's words," "Whatever My Father says to do, that's what I'm going to do; whatever My Father says to say, that's what I'm going to say." In like manner, the Spirit is subordinate to the Father and the Son. Both the Father and the Son send forth the Spirit. Should we then conclude that somehow the Second Person of the Trinity is less than the Father in terms of dignity, power, and glory, or that God the Holy Spirit is somewhat lacking, at least in comparison to the Father and the Son, in holiness, graciousness, or sovereignty? Of course not.

We need to understand that as the Father is making these assignments in the covenant of redemption, He is not doing so on the basis of particular strengths or weaknesses. It's not as though He is thinking, "Well, you know the Son has always been so good at being self-less. I'll incarnate Him. And don't I do wrath well? And the Spirit, He's a sweet guy. Let's have Him do the indwelling part." No, the roles are not assigned on the basis of differences among the members of the Trinity, simply because there aren't any differences. There is no attribute or perfection that you can predicate to one member of the Trinity that you cannot likewise predicate of all the members of the Trinity. In their being, they are the same.

And this helps us understand the relationship between

husbands and wives. When Paul commands wives to submit to their husbands as unto the Lord, he is not saying wives are less important, that they're less valuable, that they are less able than their husbands. Wives need to understand this, lest they wilt under this command. And husbands must understand this lest they lord it over their wives. God didn't say, "Well, the husbands are the smarter, stronger, wiser, more godly ones. Therefore I'll put them in charge." Rather we are talking about roles. This is about what we are called to do, not about what we are.

There is yet another important qualifier to this passage. Paul tells us that wives are to submit to their own husbands. This is not an issue having to do with the relationship between men and women, but between husbands and wives. Paul does not teach that all men have authority over all women, or that all women must submit to all men. It is quite clear that such is not the case. Wives cannot submit to other men, because they must submit to their own husbands. No one can serve two masters. That means I can't pick out just any woman and say, "I want you to make me some bacon and eggs," and if she refuses, then answer, "I'm a man, and you are a woman, so get busy." I am a man, but only one woman has been called to be submissive to me—my dear wife.

Then there is a third appropriate qualification. As we've seen, wives are commanded to submit to their own husbands "as to the Lord." We've already mentioned the four different institutions that God has created: individuals, families, states, and churches. Remember also that God has established tools for exercising authority in each of these institutions. The individual is governed by the conscience. Children in the family are ruled by the rod. The state rules through the sword. And the church rules through the power of the keys, the exercise of church discipline. Each of these exist as aids to our obedience to the one true authority, God Himself.

But there is a problem. Each of these God-ordained hierarchies involves people who are not Jesus, who are not sinless. Nevertheless, here we have the command to wives that they must submit to their own husbands as unto the Lord. That is both a description of the submission and a restriction on that submission. Remember what happened when John and Peter were commanded by those in authority to cease preaching in the name of Christ? Their response was at the same time simple and profound: "Whether it is right in the sight of God to listen to you rather than to God, you must judge" (Acts 4:19). There is a limitation to all authority, save the authority of God Himself. None of the authorities that He has established can command us to do what He forbids or forbid us to do what He commands.

If, for instance, I were to say to my dear wife, "I want you to walk down to the First National Bank. When you get there, blow up the safe door, walk in, and take all the cash you can find. I'm thinking about buying a new camper." Suppose then my wife responds, "Well, I'm not sure I can do that." I cannot then instruct her, "Look—turn in your Bible to Ephesians 5." Her duty would be to disobey me and to obey God's injunction against stealing. This, you understand, is not an invitation to anarchy, a blank check that qualifies this command out of existence. Peter never said to the authorities, "I will have no government over me except God." We can recognize legitimate authority even when we disobey its illegitimate command to do what God forbids.

Our next qualifier is perhaps the most difficult and is built once again around this concluding phrase, "as to the Lord." That phrase not only tells us that there are circumstances where wives must not obey their husbands, but also tells us, when they obey, with what spirit they ought to obey. A begrudging obedience is no obedience at all. We as the church do not respond to the Lord's commands, "Well, if You say we have to do it, we suppose we have to do it." The submission of a wife to her husband ought to reflect the same joy that we are called to in our submission to our King.

But there is a third point we ought not to miss about that pregnant phrase, "as to the Lord." This, as with all that we have looked at, ties back into the dominion mandate. That is, it is important for husbands to remember for what goal they are working. The purpose behind the submission of the wife is not so that we who are husbands might enjoy the benefits of a personal servant. Paul isn't saying here, "Now you wives—this is what I want you to do: When your husband gets home, I want you to have him lie on a bunch of pillows while you fan him with a palm frond and drop dried figs into his mouth." Rather, this submission has to do with the goal of the exercise of dominion, for the building of the kingdom. Husbands and wives are working together, the wife submissive to the husband, toward the grand and glorious goal of making manifest the reign of Christ.

As with the members of the Trinity, while there is an equality of value but a distinction of authority, there is also a distinction in calling. While husbands and wives work together in the building of the kingdom, their work is not identical. We see something of this in Paul's letter to Titus where he writes, "Older women likewise are to be reverent in behavior, not slanderers or slaves to much wine. They are to teach what is good, and so train the young women to love their husbands and children, to be self-controlled, pure, working at home, kind, and submissive to their own husbands, that the word of God may not be reviled" (2:3-4). We already considered together the baleful propensity in the culture, and in the church, to tear families apart, to divide people into demographic groups. The above passage is one of the very few places in Scripture where God Himself makes demographic distinctions. He talks about older women, and He talks about younger women. What is different is that God doesn't separate them but brings them together. God charges the older women to teach the younger women to be godly wives and mothers, to tend the garden that is the home.

This passage, as with Ephesians 5, tends to draw "Yes, buts . . ." in our day. We complain that this homeward calling is not challenging, it's not glamorous, it's not important, it's not profitable. And surely if it is none of those things, it cannot be God's calling! But this again is avoiding the authority of God Himself. Paul instructed Titus to instruct the older women to instruct the younger women to be homemakers, which means that this calling comes from God Himself. That means not only that we must obey, but that it is in fact important. If it comes from God, it cannot be any more important, it cannot be any more glamorous, it cannot be any more profitable.

Only the devil could convince us as men and women to look at this call as demeaning. Both husband and wife are called to build the kingdom. Men have the principal call of going out into the jungle and turning it into the garden. Women have the principal call to tend that which is the garden. Which means this—women have the blessing of focusing their energies on raising up godly seed. Even the world, when it sees the importance of this, says, "He who rocks the cradle rules the world." My job requires me to be hunched over a computer or proofs. My wife gets to spend her time laboring in God's vineyard on that which we know will last forever, our covenant children.

Of course, these lines are not utterly distinct. I'm very much involved in the lives of my children, and in fact will answer for my labors in raising them in the nurture and admonition of the Lord. But the sum and substance of my wife's work is the children. What she is working on will never go out of print. What she's working on likewise talks back and gives hugs and kisses and says, "Mommy, I love you." That's a glorious calling.

But I'm afraid once again, because we have allowed the world to so shape our thinking that we miss the glory. We in the church have bought into feminism, not principally because women rebelled against the authority of their husbands, but because husbands haven't valued the beauty of the call to be a wife and mother. Men are the ones who have treated homemaking as unimportant, insignificant. This is utter foolishness. This is self-destruction. When we buy into the modern myth that meaning for women is found outside the home, we are distracted from the business of building the kingdom. We are living in the center of the curse upon Eve— namely, that her desire would be for her husband.

If we would be godly families, we need a spirit of rebellion, a spirit that says to the wisdom of this world, "We will not have you to rule over us." We need a thorough reformation, one that sees the beauty of the call to homemaking. May God grant us the grace to have the courage to stand against the world and in so doing to bring honor to our Husband, Jesus Christ.

5

THE COVENANT CHILD

God has not only been gracious to me in giving me such a wonderful wife, but He has graced both of us with six wonderful children, so far. My dear wife and I homeschool our children, and so I have given some thought to what I want to teach them. Though not all our children are "school age," all of our children are schooled. They are all taught by my wife and me. The center of all that we teach, of course, is God's Word. I want my children to master the content of Scripture. The Bible alone is altogether true. But even this doesn't quite narrow things down enough for very small children. While we in some sense begin their education in Genesis, the book of beginnings, the first Scripture passage we hide in their hearts is not found until the New Testament. No, we do not begin with John 3:16. From the time the children learn to speak, we begin teaching them, "Children, obey your parents in the Lord, for this is right" (Ephesians 6:1). I pray that what motivates us is not simply that we want our children to refrain from causing us trouble in their disobedience. Rather we begin here because this is the center of God's calling in the life of children. This—obeying Mommy and Daddy—is what God calls children to do. And, as with the issue of wives submitting to their own husbands, this passage ought to be perfectly clear.

Easy to understand and easy to obey, however, are two radically different things. Ironically, one of the reasons my children commit this passage to memory so well is because they hear it so often in the context of their disobedience. When one of our children disobeys, the process of discipline begins by taking the child to a private place. There I look at the child and ask, "What does God say?" That is their cue. They know they are to respond, and they always do, "Children, obey your parents in the Lord, for this is right." They do not puzzle over it. They have not forgotten it. Still, though, they seem often to find it easy to disobey it.

There is a reason for this disobedience to the clear, uncomplicated command of God. My children come by their disobedience naturally. You see, their daddy is not only a daddy, but a child. I have a heavenly Father. He has commanded that I should obey Him at all times and in all circumstances. But I don't always obey Him. Of course, I too come by this naturally. My own earthly father has the same problem. Our children disobey us, and in doing so they disobey God because they are sinners. And they are sinners because we are sinners. Sinning is easy. Obedience is tough.

But we need to not lose sight of what is easy here in this passage. There is a simplicity to the command of Paul here. There is one charge to the children, not dozens of them. Paul doesn't say that the call of children is to get straight A's at school, to be the captain of the football team, and to obey parents. Neither does Paul write to the children, "This is what I want you to do—I want you to clarify your values. It is vital that you wrestle with the great ethical conundrums of our day, and when, having done so, you emerge with the right answers, then you'll know what to do." God doesn't burden children in this way. What does God require of the child? That they obey their parents in the Lord.

This is what children were made for. Just as with the struggle wives have in submitting to their own husbands, so here the tension is between our created nature and our fallen nature. It is because we are sinners that we sin. It is because they are sinners that our children find it difficult to obey. But as children, in their back-to-the-garden nature, they were designed to follow. As we help them learn to obey, we are leading them back to their original nature, and away from their fallen nature.

Of course we need to remember again that, just as husbands sin, so too do parents sin. That is, the authority of parents has a limit here. How are children to obey their parents? "In the Lord." The principle is the same as with the wife. It is the duty of children to obey their parents unless or until the parent forbids the child to do what God commands or commands the child to do what God forbids. If I were to say to my son, "Campbell, I want you to go down and rob the bank because I need a new truck to pull my new camper," he must not respond, "Well, I'm a child, and therefore I am not responsible. My duty to obey God leads me only to my duty to obey my father. I will go rob the bank." While surely in such a scenario my guilt would outweigh my son's guilt, nevertheless his duty would be to disobey my orders, in obedience to God.

The difficulty with this section of Ephesians 6 is not in the instruction Paul gives to the children. Rather, the hard part is when Paul turns his attention back to the parents, especially to the fathers. Paul goes on, "'Honor your father and your mother' (this is the first commandment with a promise), 'that it may go well with you and that you may live long in the land'" (vv. 2-3). By the way, the second verse my children learn is Exodus 20:12, which Paul quotes here. They get a double whammy of God's call to children to honor and obey their parents. Then Paul goes on, "Fathers, do not provoke your children to anger, but bring them up in the discipline and instruction of the Lord" (v. 4).

Isn't it interesting how swiftly Paul moves from addressing the children to addressing the fathers? I believe this is still more evidence of what we looked at earlier. The father is indeed the king in his home, which means he is responsible for all that goes on in the home. He will answer for his labors in teaching the children to obey their parents. This is a burden on fathers, but one that we cannot escape.

That doesn't mean, however, that we don't try to escape. Fathers have their own version of the "Yes, but . . ." problem. But this "but" is right there in the text. We fathers are not to provoke our children to wrath, but to bring them up in the training and admonition of the Lord. What do we do with this "but"? We turn it upside down. We think that Paul is essentially telling fathers, "Fathers, you need to make sure that your children obey. But be careful not to overdo it. You know what happens when you are too strict with the children, don't you? It causes them to rebel. What you need to do is leave some room in which your children can go out and sin and disobey. Give them free rein when they turn two. Expect them to be rebellious in their teens. Don't clamp down or it will only make things worse."

This understanding of this passage is not only bad exegesis, it is bad grammar. We do not want to provoke our children to wrath. How do we make sure we don't do that? By raising them in the training and admonition of the Lord.

What is the opposite of not provoking your children to wrath? Making sure that they obey. Indeed, we provoke our children to wrath when we do not make sure that they obey. What brings the wrath is not our thoroughness in raising the children in the training and admonition of the Lord, but our sloppiness. Our job as fathers is here again crystal-clear—to raise the children in the training and admonition of the Lord. We are not called to find some happy medium between obedience and disobedience. We're not called to command some obedience, but not too much.

How do you provoke your children to wrath? You do it first by failing to discipline them. Part of the discipline process in our home is making sure the children remember why we are doing it. After a spanking I will often ask my children, "Why did Daddy spank you?" Their response is always the same: "To help me learn to obey." And I will then remind the child of another passage: "Folly is bound up in the heart of a child, but the rod of discipline drives it far from them" (Proverbs 22:15). This conversation also serves to remind me and the children that I too am a man under authority. I spank because I am not to disobey my heavenly Father.

We live in a world that tells us that the rod is bad. We have experts writing learned papers for prestigious journals telling us that when we spank our children we train them to be violent. We are told that spanking damages our children. So we tend to accommodate the wisdom of the world. We believe the "child-rearing experts" rather than He who created the children in the first place. We think maybe instead of giving us the rod as a tool of enforcement, God gave us the time-out chair. And in so doing we make manifest our own disobedience. We likewise make manifest our own hatred for our children (Proverbs 13:24). I do not need to make a case for using the rod. Here too the Bible is abundantly clear.

Why do we spank? Why do we train our children to obey, and why do we punish them when they don't? This is not a side issue, but the very substance of our child-rearing. We do not punish our children retributively. To put it more plainly, we do not punish our children for the sake of bringing justice to pass. That's not our goal. There are not only different spheres of authority, complete with different tools of enforcement, but there are also different goals, different purposes for punishment. The call of the state is to use the sword as a tool of justice. But it is not justice I seek in disciplining my children. Why not? Because if my children are God's children, then justice has already been done, in mercy. If my children are His children, than the retributive justice due to my children for their disobedience was put upon Christ in His passion. Retribution was made at Calvary.

The function of the punishment is to train my children in obedience. It is rehabilitative rather than punitive. I explain to my children that I am not spanking them in order to make things right, to even out the scales of justice. Rather I am spanking them because I want to make *them* right. That's my motivation in spanking my children, and that's also why it ought to be for us such a joyous occasion.

One of the most common ways that we provoke our children to wrath is that we too often discipline them in our wrath. When we do this we are essentially saying to our children, "I'm angry at you, and I'm going to vent that anger in your punishment." When we do this we are confused not only in how we punish, but why we do it. I tend to look rather silly when I'm about the business of disciplining my children. I get a big goofy grin on my face, looking to all the world like some kind of twisted sadist. My biggest frustration is not when my children commit rank rebellion, but when they walk that line between obedience and rebellion. I hate trying to figure it out, to wrestle over what I'm supposed to do. But when the disobedience is blatant and clear, then of course my calling is likewise clear. And that provides a powerful opportunity to train my children.

This is how discipline progresses in our home when I am doing it right. Suppose, for the sake of argument, that my son Campbell has shoved his sister Delaney. How would I know this? Delaney would come to me and say, "Daddy, Campbell shoved me." I pray that the reason she comes to me is because she knows I need to know these things. I fear she may be struggling with delighting in the misery of another. My response is calm and measured. "Please go and tell Campbell to come see me in his room, and tell him to pick up the spanking stick on his way." Delaney will be tempted to ask me, "Is he going to get a spanking?" But soon she will learn my standard response to such questions: "It's not your concern."

Campbell enters the room with the spanking stick, and I ask, "Campbell, did you shove your sister?"

"Yes, Daddy."

"Has Daddy told you that boys are to protect girls?"

"Yes, Daddy."

"Is shoving your sister protecting girls?"

"No, Daddy."

"What does God say, son?"

"Children, obey your parents in the Lord, for this is right."

"That's right, son, and you disobeyed Daddy. Daddy, who must obey God, must spank you. Why is Daddy going to spank you?"

"To help me learn to obey."

At this point I bend Campbell over my knee and give him a thorough *swack!* with the spanking stick, and then comes the best part of all. What does Campbell do? He jumps up and wraps his arms around my neck, clinging to me as he says, "I'm sorry, Daddy." And I say, "Campbell, Daddy forgives you, and Daddy loves you." And I hold him, and I hold him, and I hold him. He squeezes me so hard. Soon his tears begin to dry up as I hold him and remind him that it's all over now. He stands up and is ready to go back out to play. But I am not finished. I look him in the eye and ask him, "Son, what is God's promise?" He replies, "If we confess our sins, he is faithful and just to forgive us our sins and to cleanse us from all unrighteousness" (1 John 1:9). The amazing thing, though, is that often, as he is reciting this passage, both his eyes and mine begin to well up again. Father and son, in the context of this discipline, have an occasion to be overwhelmed by the grace of God. We enjoy a gospel party. "Isn't it grand, son? Isn't it glorious?" I'll ask him.

We finish our discipline with a prayer. Campbell remembers to pray three things. First, he asks that God would forgive him for his sin. Second, he thanks God that His Son died on the cross that his sins might be forgiven. Third, he asks God that He would help Campbell to grow in grace, to be more obedient. Please note, by the way, that such a prayer isn't just for children. It is the appropriate response when anyone sins.

We provoke our children to wrath when we punish them in our anger, when we punish them retributively. We likewise provoke our children to wrath when we fail to discipline them, because we want to be their buddy. I love my children, all six of them. I delight to spend time with them and am eager to finish this chapter so that I can go and be with them. We play together and have great fun together. But I am always Daddy. I am always the authority in our home (and my authority backs up the authority of my dear wife). I am the head of my home, and my children are always conscious of that, and in fact are comforted by it. Your children don't want you to be their buddy. They have buddies. Instead they look to you for protection, not only from others, not only from brothers who shove them, but from themselves. They want to know that you're there to protect them from themselves.

Our calling when we discipline our children is to do so not because we're angry, not because we're embarrassed, but because we long to see our children grow in obedience. Do you love your children? Do you want it to go well with them on the earth? Then what do you do? You exercise your authority in the exercise of discipline. You do not provoke your children to wrath, but you bring them up in the training and admonition of the Lord. Though it isn't always a part of the liturgy of our discipline, I often remind my children of this point as well. Sometimes when I discipline one of my children I'll say, "You know why Daddy does this. Daddy wants you to be happy, and if you want to be happy you need to be blessed, and if you want to be blessed you must grow in your obedience to God. Daddy does this because Daddy loves you."

Your children will trust you on this; they will believe you on this as you remain faithful to it. It is important to remember that Paul's admonition is rather specific. The last part of verse 4, "the discipline and instruction of the Lord" is sometimes translated "nurture and admonition," sometimes "fear and admonition." The Greek word that is translated "discipline" or "training" or "nurture" or "fear" is *paideia*. The root of this word is grounded in the idea of culture. What Paul is enjoining here is that we would bring our children up in the culture of the Lord. Throughout this book we have seen how the serpent seeks to get us to think his thoughts after him. He wants your children to look at God, at themselves, at their families, at the world around them in a certain way. But God, in making covenant with families, tells us that our job as parents is to raise them in His world, in His culture, in His kingdom, on His side in the great battle between the Seed of the woman and the seed of the serpent.

That's what the *shema*, the most sacred text of the whole Bible to the Old Testament Jews, is all about: "Hear, O Israel. The LORD our God, the Lord is one. You shall love the LORD your God with all your heart and with all your soul and with all your might" (Deuteronomy 6:4-5). What comes next? "And these words that I command you today shall be on your heart. You shall teach them diligently to your children, and shall talk of them when you sit in your house, and when you walk by the way, and when you lie down, and when you rise" (vv. 6-7). God is telling His people to teach the children, teach the children, teach the children. Tell them who God is, what God has done, and what God requires of us. That's what it means to raise them in God's culture, and what a glorious culture it is. Our lives, ourselves, and our children are all about the glory of the kingdom of God.

Our family tradition begins at birth. When God blesses us with a daughter, which He has now done five times, after she is cleaned up, after Mommy gets to hold her, after they wrap her up tight like a loaf of bread, the nurses always put the baby in the tiny little bassinette on wheels with a heat lamp. That's when it's my turn. I take my Bible and go to my daughter and speak these first words to her: "Darby" (or Shannon or Delaney or Erin Claire or Maili), "this is Daddy, and I want to read something to you." I open my Bible to Proverbs 31, to that beautiful portrait of a godly woman, and read it. "This," I then explain to my minutes-old little girl, "is your calling. This is what Mommy and Daddy will be training you to be." My son received essentially the same talk, except that I read to him from Proverbs 3.

The training continues as we teach our children their first song. You are probably familiar with it. It goes, "Father Abraham had many sons. Many sons had Father Abraham. I am one of them, and so are you. So let's just praise the Lord." What am I teaching my children? I'm giving them their identity. I'm telling them of their culture, that we are the children of Abraham, that the Bible is not just our rule book, but it is also our family history. I am telling my children that it was their great-great-great-great, I don't know how many greats, grandfather, Noah, whom God spoke to, whom God told to build an ark.

I'm giving my children an identity separate from the one established for them by pop culture. I'm giving them the identity that we share together as one family, because we are together in covenant with God. We do much the same thing in what we like to call our family liturgy. It goes something like this. I will ask those of my children who can speak, "What is your name?" They give me their first name. "What is your other name?" They then give me their second name. "What is your last name?" They answer, "Sproul." Then I ask them, "What are Sprouls?" And they reply, "Sprouls are free." Do my children have a profound understanding of freedom? Of course not. They are little children. But they will grow into that knowledge because they have been taught this is their identity.

I ask them next, "Whom do Sprouls fear?" And they reply with gusto, "Sprouls fear no man—Sprouls fear God." This is our ontology, our being. This is what we are, all of us. Finally I ask them, "Whom do Sprouls serve?" They respond, "Sprouls serve King Jesus."

I am called to raise my children in the culture of the Lord. That means I must teach my children who they are. I must explain to them their identity, and that their identity is the same as my identity and their mother's identity. In so doing I am instructing them on how to live within God's culture. I'm giving them a vision for building God's kingdom.

But our culture and our calling is not restrained to just one or two generations. I constantly remind my children that it is not enough for them to keep some of the stipulations of the covenant. It isn't enough for them to obey part of God's law. They in turn must also keep this part of the covenant—they must teach these same truths to their own children. To live in the culture is to raise children in the culture, and to raise them to do the same with their children. Our identity then transcends this generation. We are the heirs of our parents, who were the heirs of their parents, who were the heirs of their parents. And in the second Adam we are heirs of all things. Our common calling, then, is to make manifest the reign of Christ, until He comes again in great glory. May God equip us to raise up godly seed in our families. May He equip our children to do the same. May He, in fact, do mighty deeds through our children, and our children's children, for the sake of His Son and His kingdom.

6

THE CHURCH FAMILY

As we have considered together the nature and calling of the covenant family, I wouldn't be surprised if some of you have felt a bit left out. I know that when I speak on these themes at conferences, there are always people wanting to know, understandably so, "How does this apply to me?" We've seen already that the world and the serpent are at war with the family. We have focused our attention on how the devil distorts our thinking about the family. But he has not only distorted our understanding of the family—he has inflicted real, lasting damage to particular families. He has succeeded in tearing apart families that are meant to be bound together. Sin, we know, brought death into the world, and death has torn families apart. But it was also sin that brought divorce into the world, and divorce tears families apart. The solution to sin—the Gospel—ironically likewise has the capacity to tear families apart, as Jesus Himself warned.

We suggested in an earlier chapter that one of the great weaknesses in our day is that our understanding of the family has essentially been reduced down to the nuclear family. As bad as this is, it is far worse that there are in our day so few families still intact at the nuclear level. There are cities in America where illegitimate births outnumber legitimate births. We have more broken families now than we ever have had in our history. This creates circumstances where it seems that people are alone, that they are no longer connected to a family. We, I hope, have seen already that the Bible has much to say to those who are bound together in families. But does the Bible speak to those who are without families? Does it address those who are family-less?

As is so often the case, the answer is yes and no. The Bible does speak to those who, because of sin, because of death, because of divorce, because even of the Gospel, are left without biological kin. It has some very specific things to say of those who are in this kind of circumstance. But the answer is also no, for those who are a part of the church, who are the children of God, the bride of Christ, cannot rightly be understood to be family-less. If you are a citizen of the kingdom of God, then you are part of a family. All Christians are in fact a part of the family of God, which is the church.

We have considered together, several times, the four institutions that God has established among men: the individual, the family, the church, and the state. We looked at how in our day the devil is seeking to expand the scope of the individual and the state and to squeeze out the mediating institutions, the family and the church. The family and the church fight a war on two fronts as the world tries to squeeze each of them out of existence.

That ought to mean, of course, that these two mediating institutions would band together, to take common cause against their common enemies. Sadly, too often what we see instead is that these two institutions squabble over what remains of the pie. While there is a vital relationship between the family and the church, too often we have melded the two together where we shouldn't have and have divided the two where we should have kept them together. As we consider these issues—where the church has intruded upon the family, and to a lesser extent where the family has intruded upon the church—we should reach some wisdom on how the church is called to relate to those who are without families.

Where are we muddled on these issues? One place we get confused on the appropriate roles for the family and the church is in the church where we follow the way of the world in terms of dividing families. Just as the world has a separate program for fathers, mothers, teenagers, children, and toddlers, too often we do the same in the church. When we separate husbands from wives, when we pull apart parents from their children, we essentially divide up the church. We no longer have one church but a tiny children's church, a men's church, and a ladies' church. We hire professionals at the church and so encourage men to abdicate their responsibilities for the spiritual growth and well-being of their families.

It also happens, however, the other way. There are families out there, many of them because they are frustrated with the attempts by local churches to divide up their families, who make the opposite error of thinking they are the church. There is a misguided but growing movement in our day of families thinking they can be churches unto themselves. This is dangerous on many fronts.

Instead the calling is this: The church ought to be, as the family of God, seeking the kingdom of God, trying to make manifest or visible the reign of Jesus Christ by being a family above the family and by being a family to the family-less.

What does it mean to be a family above the family? We've looked several times at the limitations on the authority God has given to those in positions of leadership. Remember that a child is to obey his or her parents "in the Lord." There is a line that must not be crossed. We must, if we are forced to choose, obey God rather than men. In like manner, when Paul in Ephesians 5 commands that wives must submit to their husbands, it is "as to the Lord." The same principle applies. No wife is to obey her husband when he insists that she violate the law of God.

This principle is founded upon the hard truth that wherever God established human authority, that human authority is beset by sin. Husbands have asked their wives to disobey God. Parents have done the same to their children. Under heaven, if there is to be authority, it will be an authority tainted by sin. But there is more to the solution than simple disobedience. Often our disputes arise when both parties insist that the law of God is on their side. Sometimes husbands fail to lead as Jesus leads. Sometimes wives fail to follow as the church is called to follow Christ. So what do we do?

Here is where the church is to be the family above the family. God has established the church in part as a sort of court of appeals. In so doing He has reminded us that all of us are under authority. The husband is indeed king in his home, but he is a king who not only reports to Jesus in a very real, spiritual way but who also reports to Jesus in a real, spiritual way through the earthly authority that Jesus established, which is the church.

How does that work in real life? Suppose that I suddenly developed an overpowering fancy for fishing. God does tell us to exercise dominion over the fish of the sea. Imagine that I enjoy fishing so much that I come to my dear wife with this idea: "You know, dear, how much I love fishing. And you know, I presume, though you do not know it in full, that I am an outstanding fisherman. You know also that there is often tension in our home about my fishing. I want to fish, while you think it more important that I cut the grass, clean the gutters, paint the house, or fix the fence. Here's my idea. I think we need to sell the house. We can take the proceeds from the sale and buy a really fine fishing boat and lots of fishing gear, and we'll move down to the lake, and I'll just fish all the time." And Denise asks, "What do you suppose we'll live in after we sell the house?" "Oh," I reply, "I have that all figured out. That's part of the beauty of the plan. We could live in a tent. Why, with the equity in our house, after the boat and the supplies, we could still afford just about the best tent there is. But it gets even better. Without the house and the yard, you won't always be asking me to do all those chores. I'll have more time to fish. Every morning I'll get up, fire up the boat, and fish all day long. What do you think?"

If I were to float this idea by my wife, she would probably respond, "Well, dear, this is not, believe it or not, the worst idea you've ever had. But it's certainly in the top three." Now suppose I conclude the discussion with, "Well, dear, you know Ephesians 5 says you are to submit to me, so I'd like you to start packing please. Call the realtor, call the banker, and I'll start looking through the classifieds for my boat." What should she do?

Our inclination, because the command is so preposterous, is to assume some sort of vague rule of thumb. We assume that Paul must mean, "Wives, submit to your own husbands unless they're out of their tree." But Paul makes no such exception. If we only submit when we agree with the wisdom of those who are in authority over us, then we never really submit at all. We're just doing what we want. So how do we help my dear wife escape? It's rather simple. All she needs to do is, and this is assuming that I refuse to hear any wisdom from her, is call our session, those who sit in the seat of authority in our local church. She calls them and asks for their help.

My wife does not have the authority to stop me from pursuing this fishing dream. But the elders of the church do have that authority. They would call me in and say, "Now, R. C., the Scripture is terribly clear that if you don't provide for your family, then you are worse than an infidel. What you are proposing to do is serious sin. The Word of God says that you must be a wise steward of what God has provided for you, and you would be a foolish steward indeed if you went through with your plans. We're here to tell you not only why we think you shouldn't do it, but to forbid you to do it. If necessary we will exercise the power of the keys. If you do not repent and turn from this wicked plan, we will excommunicate you from the church of Christ."

This is what a court of appeals is supposed to do. My wife and I have a dispute. We are not agreeing. I am asking her to do something she doesn't think she ought to do. So she goes to court. The court she comes to, however, is the church, not the state. That I am not Jesus is painfully apparent. But here, in a church that is willing to exercise discipline, that recognizes its rightful calling in these circumstances, she has protection. If we were in a church that lacked this mark of the true church, discipline, my poor wife would be on her own.

But there is a limit going in the other direction as well. Those who exercise authority in the church need to be careful. Suppose instead of planning to buy a tent and fish the rest of my life, I come home to my dear wife one day and say, "You know, I was down in Florida, and I saw the neatest thing. There were several homes there that had—you won't believe this—it was just so beautiful, stunning. Right there, in their front yards where you could see them when you drove by, they had these really huge, plastic, big pink flamingoes. They were so cool. On my way back to Virginia I stopped and picked up a dozen for our yard. Boy, will our neighbors be jealous." Now what happens when my wife, already embarrassed by the way her husband dresses, goes to the session in the hopes of avoiding further embarrassment?

I suppose my session would laugh, understanding the trials my wife goes through because of my lack of taste. But then they might say, "You know, Denise, as much as we sympathize with you, this is not the appropriate jurisdiction for this issue. This is just not that significant of an issue to warrant our stepping in. We're sorry that you're going to have to live with a tacky yard. You've gotten used to his ties not matching his shirt. You can get used to this as well. You're going to have to get over this."

Like any court, the court of appeals that is the local session at the church cannot afford to be bogged down with frivolous "lawsuits" among family members. In fact, when they do get involved in these petty issues, what will happen is they will micromanage the home and leave precious little room for the husband to exercise his God-given authority. Families need to be able to work these things out. Sometimes submission may mean having to put up with petty quirks and weaknesses.

Do not let all this court language, however, confuse you. Remember as we looked earlier at the nature of covenants that we argued that covenants are in some ways like contracts, but in other ways they are more akin to relationships. In fact, the beauty of the covenant is that it marries together the legal and the familial. When we reduce things down to contracts, we've lost something. If I were intent on fishing for the rest of my life, the session wouldn't send me a cold and professional subpoena telling me, "You will appear before this court on such and such a date." Instead they might say to me, "Brother R. C., our friend, for whom we care, to whom we have covenanted, let's talk about this plan of yours. Please hear the wisdom of the elders."

Of course, on the other hand we cannot err on the side of too much family and not enough contract. If I refuse to hear wisdom, it isn't enough for the older gentlemen in the church to simply say, "We think your plan isn't such a good one" and leave it at that. We ought not to split asunder what the covenant has brought together. We need both the enforcing of the law and the tender care of the family.

The church is not only called to be a family above the family—it is also called to be a family to those who have no family. Scripture speaks of these folks, and we would do well to recover the language of the Bible. The Bible calls those without family "widows and orphans." If we simply remembered that, we would not only see that the Bible does in fact address these people, but that we are called to show forth to them an extra measure of grace.

Paul wrote to Timothy, "Honor widows who are truly widows. But if a widow has children or grandchildren, let them first learn to show godliness to their own household and to make some return to their parents, for this is pleasing in the sight of God" (1 Timothy 5:3-4). What is Paul saying? Is he guilty of redundancy or doubletalk when he writes of widows who are really widows? How can one be a widow without being a widow? Paul is distinguishing two different kinds of widows. On the one hand are those who yet have other family. They have no husbands, but they do have families. This is the first line of defense. Of course, here is one place the state has crept into an arena in which it does not belong. Widows in our day are instructed to turn to the state for their care. Not so according to the Bible. First it is the extended family.

The second group of widows, widows indeed, are those who have no extended family. These were women with no husband and no family. And Paul's instructions are rather clear here: The church must be a family to the widow. If possible, the solution is to help the widow become a non-widow, that she might remarry. I am puzzled over why we don't see this happening too often in the church.

If remarriage, however, is out of the question, this is where the church steps in. The church becomes the family to the family-less. We are to care for these women, tend to them, take care of their needs. The Bible, however, not only tells us what we are to do here, but also tells us how important it is that we do this. James tells us, "Religion that is pure and undefiled before God and the Father is this: to visit orphans and widows in their affliction, and to keep oneself unstained from the world" (James 1:27). I'm afraid we fail to visit orphans and widows in their trouble precisely because we are spotted by the world. James is telling us here that this is not a peripheral matter. We cannot slough off these duties and still claim to be within the one true faith. This is not an option; yet I'm afraid we as the church rarely fulfill this mandate.

I understand how difficult this can be. The church that I serve, Saint Peter Presbyterian Church, is a rather small church. When we were confronted with this situation, we were a tiny little church. We had a young married couple in our congregation with two small children. After about four years of marriage, the husband decided he had had enough, and so packed his bags and left. The session of the church called upon the man to repent of his sin. He refused, and so in due time he was excommunicated from the church. He was told that as far as we were concerned, he was dead to us unless or until he repented. At this time our church didn't even have ten families, and now one of them was without a husband and father. Not only that, but the infidel father, from the time he left, even to this day as far as I know, did not send a single dime to support his wife and children.

What could we do? Our session met and reasoned together, "We're a tiny, struggling church. We're barely past being a mission church. We have hardly any families, hardly any money. But God tells us precisely what we are supposed to do. We will care for this woman and her dear children. That's what we must do." We ended up buying a trailer. We put the woman and her children in that trailer and told her, "You send us the bills. We will pay for your groceries, your lot rent, your phone, electricity, water; whatever you need, we as a church will pay for it. That's what we're called to do."

It happened, in the providence of God, that the trailer we bought was right next to one owned by another family in the church. The wife of that family was quite friendly with that "widow," and the husband was a fine, godly young man. The session gave him a job to do. When the widow needed a drain unclogged, it was his duty to get it done. In the evenings, when he gathered his own small family together for family worship, he was to include the widow and her children. When the children were unresponsive to the discipline of the mother, he was to exercise discipline there as well. He was to be a father and a husband to this family in very ordinary, practical, and natural ways. Because of his character, he was able and willing to perform these duties. And in doing so he modeled for the little boy what a godly man acted like.

Word got out about what we were doing for this family. It did not surprise us that the world was stunned by our decision. We didn't expect them to understand our convictions. What astonished our church, however, was how we surprised the other churches in the area. One would have thought we in our church were little green men from Mars. We were asked, "What are you doing? Are you insane?" That ended up being perhaps the hardest part of what we went through, accepting the incredulity of too many churches around us. Of course we were encouraged as well, as many churches also helped us carry the load financially.

It was a hard thing for the widow. We weren't, of course, able to keep her in great style. She, of course, had to trust that the church would meet her needs. The state offered to do the same. She had to choose one or the other, because we as a church had no interest in helping the state care for her. It was tough on her pride. But I reminded her that her calling at that time was to be Jesus to us, that we might have the opportunity to be Jesus to her. We cannot give a cup of water in the name of Christ unless there are those in our midst who have need of a cup of water. He called her to be thirsty, that He might call us to give her drink.

One need not wait, of course, for needs to get quite this dramatic. I venture to guess that each of us, somewhere in our home church, have those who, if not being widows indeed, are at least not overflowing to abundance in terms of family. There are single women who might need to have a flat tire changed. There are older women who might need to have their lawn mowed from time to time. There is no reason churches cannot go and become fathers to the fatherless, husbands to the husbandless. In fact, there is every reason for us to do so. It's not terribly complicated. The widows will be pleased, the orphans will be pleased, and the world will be shocked. Not least God commands it, and God likewise will reward our obedience.

I told our widow that as hard as it was on her, it was a delight for us as a church to meet her needs and the needs of her precious children. It was a delight because of our genuine love for her and for them. We had vowed when she joined the church to love her. We had vowed when her children were baptized to aid her in raising them in the nurture and admonition of the Lord. We had no choice. But as is so often the case, obedience was for us a joy. No experience in the short life thus far of our church has more tightly bound us together as the body of Christ.

My prayer is that such will happen all across the spectrum within the church of Christ. Let us by all means recover what James calls "pure and undefiled . . . religion." This is not a substitute for the Gospel of Jesus Christ, but its necessary outworking. May the Spirit who gives us life give us the grace to be families to those who are without families, that our heavenly Father would be pleased.

7

QUESTIONS AND ANSWERS

In this last chapter, my father, R. C. Sproul, Sr., dialogues with me about homeschooling, which my wife and I have found to be a great tool and gift from the Lord, and an important part of our family life. In the process we discuss key issues of family life and God's design for our families.

As with the introduction to this book, in the dialogue that follows, the comments of the father (R. C. Sproul, Sr.) appear in roman type, those of the son (R. C. Sproul, Jr.) in italics.

One of the main questions to come out of your talks has to do with the phenomenon that I never, in my wildest dreams, could ever have imagined would take place in the United States of America, and that's the homeschool movement, with today literally millions of children taken out of the public school system by their parents, or even out of the Christian school system. These parents have taken upon themselves the responsibility of teaching their children at home. I know that you and Denise are involved in that enterprise of homeschooling, and I'd like to know, is this something you choose to do solely as a personal preference, or do you recommend this for other people?

Well, I would probably answer the latter to that. It is definitely something that I recommend; in fact, it's not at all unusual for me to speak at homeschooling conferences and such. I recognize that different families are in different circumstances and different situations, and I affirm that there might be, in some circumstances, better choices for other particular families. The benefits of homeschooling are, to my mind, just astounding. In doing that we not only have, of course, the freedom and the duty to instill in our children all that we've been talking about—to raise them in the culture of God—but everything we teach is taught in the context of the authority of God and the authority of God's Word. Not only do we have prayer, not only do we read the Bible, not only can we meet at the pole, so to speak, but every moment of every day when we're teaching our children, we're teaching them the context of all truth belonging to and coming from the one true God, the God of the Bible, which is something you can't do in the public school system.

Do you think there's such a thing, R. C., as a neutral educational curriculum?

Absolutely not. Of course, it depends on what you mean by neutral. If you mean by neutral, true, yes, this is the Christian way of doing things. But we have this tendency to think that if we teach our children the Christian faith or teach them whatever we're teaching them in the context of the authority of God, somehow we're not being fair.

Or we're not being really academically honest.

Right.

Some would say we're not being disassociated and detached from the evidence. We're propagandizing our children or inculcating them in a religious viewpoint, whereas the public school doesn't do that.

That's the accusation. And of course everybody does come from a particular point of view—in the public school, in the homeschool, in the Christian school. And what we're doing, what we're saying, is that we believe this is true. This is why we do this.

In other words, if you teach mathematics from the perspective of the sovereignty of God, that's one perspective; and if you said, "God has nothing to do with mathematics," that's a different perspective. Each is a theological position.

Exactly. It's religious. I had the opportunity several years ago to participate in a panel discussion at a conference on the issue of the relationship of children and public schools. One of the men on the panel, Bill Spady, who's known as the father of outcome-based education, was given the task of trying to persuade the Christians in the audience that their children were safe in public schools. He argued that the public school is not interested in undoing our children's convictions—that outcome-based education is all about choices, and they just want to lay down choices. In outcome-based education they don't want to say no to any point of view. That's why our children are safe with them, they say.

Now, my job was to respond to his talk. So I stood up, and I said, "I'm a Christian. I'm a Reformed Christian. I'm a Presbyterian, Reformed Christian. I'm a Reformed, Presbyterian, postmillennial Christian." I added about thirty qualifiers about my convictions, and then I said, "Every morning when I wake up, my job is to teach my children all of those things. And every night when I go to bed, I pray that they will learn these things because the reason I am all these things is because I believe all these things to be true. So don't tell me you want to give my children choices. My job is not to give my children choices. My job is to teach my children the truth, and homeschooling does that more than any other option. I recognize that not all Christians, my brothers and sisters in Christ, share all the convictions in my long list of qualifiers, and I am to love them. But in my homeschool, I get to give my children what I believe."

This outcome-based concept of education is really a thinly veiled form of relativism, isn't it?

It's not even veiled. It's really pretty obvious. So I think homeschooling is the ideal choice. I think, again, that in some circumstances it would be better for parents to put their children in a Christian school. Also I understand that when I teach my children, I am never their only teacher. The second I hand my child a book, I bring other views into the equation—unless it's one of my books, of course. Please understand, I don't want to draw some hard and fast line. In fact, one of the things that I do is to teach homeschooled high schoolers. We have a little academy that meets once a week, and I teach a few classes. I'm not against that, and because I'm not against that, I don't want to say, "No, you can't go to Christian school." But I do think that the more control and authority you have over the rearing of your own children, the better off you, and they, are.

Well, R. C., you know that before we even began Ligonier Ministries over thirty years ago, I had a personal friendship with Francis Schaeffer, and in fact I had several consultations with him regarding the founding of Ligonier Ministries. We carried on a personal friendship until he died. And about twenty years ago he and I were both sharing a platform at a theological seminary where we were both speaking, and we met each other at the airport in that particular city and shared a cab ride from the airport to our hotel. I remember that particular encounter with Fran because I asked him on the way, "What is your greatest concern right now about the Christian community in the United States?" He did not hesitate. His immediate response was, "Statism." You didn't mention much about that fourth category, but what he meant by statism was not simply that we have a government—a free government, even a good government, and we're patriotic and loyal and all that—he was concerned with the word *state* with those three letters put on the end of it—*ism*.

Rightly so.

He was identifying an ideology where our meaning and existence are defined in terms of the state.

Which is more than ideology. It's a religion.

Yes, and I've noticed a change in nomenclature in the last decade or so. Though we used to customarily describe the secular educational systems as public education—the public school system, which was a part of the fabric of American tradition—in the last ten years we've heard it more often called government schools because there's been a much greater centralization, a much greater involvement in curriculum planning and the government of the school system by the secular state. And we've also seen a growing hostility toward anything Christian included in that realm. Again, what Schaeffer was saying to me was not that his biggest concern for America as a *nation* was statism. His biggest concern for *the church* in America was statism.

Right.

I've often wondered what he would say if he were here today to see his concerns having come to fruition, and I think part of the response of the homeschool movement is Christian parents' saying, "This far, no further. We're going to take control. We're going to recover our children."

When we ask the state or even permit the state to educate

our children, even if their teachers love the Christian faith, we're already guilty of responsibility drift. That is, God has given parents this obligation. Now again, there may be a degree to which we can delegate this to someone outside the home . . .

In loco parentis.

But you can't delegate it to a whole different alien institution like the state because all education is inherently religious.

A few years ago I did a series of lectures in nations that had just come out of the Iron Curtain environment. I was in what was then Czechoslovakia. I lectured for a week in Prague, and then I went to Budapest for a week of lectures, and then on to Romania. This was very shortly after the great breakdown of the Soviet Union, and what I most remember about that trip were conversations I had with Christians in Hungary as I was asking them about the Hungarian Revolution in the fifties and the Russian tanks and the kids with the stones and all of that, and they were telling me horror stories. They were telling me that the school set up a kind of system requiring the children to tell the school officials if their parents tried to pray with them at home. But the Christian parents continued to pray, and they told their children, "You must not tell this to your schoolteachers, because we could go to jail or we could be killed." I can't imagine that could happen in the world in our day, but I guess that shows how naive I am. But people need to really be careful about that.

But here's a question with respect to homeschooling, a common question, I think. I'm sure you've heard it many times. Some say that homeschooling is the most biblical way of teaching children; however, homeschooled children are, to a certain degree, isolated from other children, from their culture, and so on. How do you prepare children who are, in a sense, sheltered from the world with the homeschool experience to be salt and light? How do you prepare them to function in a strange and foreign land?

Well, you know that is a gracious way of asking the question. A lot of times when people are unhappy with the idea of homeschooling, they make the accusation, "You're sheltering your children," and I have a prepackaged response to that. "What are you going to accuse me of next, feeding and clothing them?"

I think it is a happy and a healthy thing to keep our children distinct from the world around them. Our problem in the church is that we think the way to be salt is to be rotten meat and the way to be light is to be darkness. We get so close to the world that we become like it. We want our children to be distinct, to be a city on a hill, not a light hidden under a bushel.

My children right now interact with people outside of our family. Another way of expressing the problem we're discussing is to refer to it as the socialization problem, the number one objection to homeschooling. And I have another answer for that. "You're concerned about socialization?" I ask, and they say, "Yes." Then I say, "And you think that means the ability to get along with people who are different?" And they say, "Well, yeah. That's a good summary." So I say, "So your solution is to lock my child in a room with kids exactly their age all day long." My children interact all day long with their younger brothers and sisters, their older brothers and sisters, their Mommy and Daddy, and people who come into our home; and when we go out into the world, and we do, with all manner of grown-ups, the grown-ups can't believe what they see. Right now we're in a place politically where I don't have to homeschool in a catacomb. I can tell people, "Yes, we homeschool our kids," and I'll tell them, "Go ahead and ask them something. Ask them the capitals of different states." "The capital of Virginia is Richmond," they answer confidently. The kids just rattle off a little of what they've learned, and some people can't believe it. We have experiences like that when we go out to eat too. We go into restaurants where there are actually unbelievers.

No.

Yes, and when we unload out of the van and start strolling in with all these kids, you can see the staff in the restaurant get a look of dread and panic. They're terrified. But when we walk out after eating, they're slapping us on the back, saying, "I can't believe this! What are you guys doing?" And we are light for the world. We say, "Look, we're showing the world that children are, in fact, a blessing." Children can be raised in the nurture and admonition of the Lord. Children can be obedient and pleasant and can have a conversation with a grown-up. And we want them to be able to do that.

Now in terms of preparing them for going out, they're already going out, and they're going out understanding that there is a difference between us (believers) and them (unbelievers). There's something in common—we're all sinners—but there's a difference—we serve King Jesus.

Let me ask you this: We always have an audience at Ligonier when we tape our programs, and I kid with our audience—I call it God's waiting room because the vast majority of people who come have been long retired, and they're up in years. And we have a great time. But not everybody in this class [Editor's note: This dialogue was originally part of a taped radio series] is in that category. We have my best student right up here in the front row—Roger. How old are you, Roger?

Thirteen.

And how long have you been coming to these tapings—three or four years?

Yes, sir.

Roger is homeschooled, and part of his homeschool curriculum is to come to these tapings, and I think he gets along great with the people in our classroom. He's a part of this classroom, and I don't think he's suffering socially.

I don't think so either.

All right, but here's the next question—I'm sure you've heard it many times. Homeschool or Christian school? Certainly homeschool requires a tremendous amount of commitment in terms of time and energy, but it also has an economic impact because it requires somebody to be home. You can't have both the mother and father working all day. And add to that the single mother who can't homeschool her child because she has to go out and earn support for the child she's taking care of. What do you say to people who have tremendous economic pressure?

Well, I want to be careful and gracious, but I think to answer the question, you have to go back further. I need to touch on one of the things that I believe about homeschooling that I even want homeschoolers to grasp—and many of them haven't yet. When I go to speak at a homeschooling conference, they often ask me, "How many children do you have?" "Six." "What are their ages?" "Nine, seven, five, four, two, and nearly one." "So you only have two or three in your homeschool?" And I say, "No, I have six in my homeschool. All of my children are in the homeschool because we're always teaching all of them."

Now in the chapter on the church and the family, I talked about how our church had a widow with two small children, and one of the reasons we took care of her needs was because she had a homeschool with her four-year-old and her two-year-old, because she had to teach them. So one of the answers, basically, is for the family to take care of these needs, and then if they can't, for the church to take care of these needs. When it comes to education, I'm so committed to not having our families choose the option of having the state educate their children that I want to be like Mother Theresa, who said on the abortion issue regarding unwanted children, "Send them to us." If you can't educate your children, move to Virginia. I'll teach your children, and I won't charge you anything because that's how important this is, and I'd love to see churches recognize this, pick up that slack, and do what God has called them to do.

Now some of these folks who cry, "Poor" aren't. Homeschooling is a sacrifice, and you certainly will have more stuff with two incomes than you will with one income. The same is true for my family.

Your wife's a certified schoolteacher, and she gave up her job to stay home and teach your kids.

Right, and I'm delighted she has done that, and that I can be involved as well. What a great reward this is—not just in terms of the future of my children, but in terms of the peace of our house and the joy in our house.

You talk about cultural ideals and the ways of the world, how in our whole culture we're taught from day one that any more than two children is a burden, and yet biblically the more children, the greater the blessing.

Right. They're gifts from God.

And people have argued, "Well, that was in an agrarian

culture, but in today's industrialized world economically more than two children is the worst curse that could befall a family." But my family is important to me. I mean, we only had two children—you and your sister; but Vesta had four miscarriages, and we would have been absolutely delighted to have had six; and the older I get, the more important to me my children are.

Of course.

There are lots of things that I enjoy in this world. I enjoy my house, but I wouldn't trade ten of those houses for one of my children.

Of course not, and the house is going to crumble and become rubble one day.

That's right.

Children last forever.

It's a value thing, isn't it?

Yeah. Let me add one more thing on how these things all relate. This is a fascinating study, going back to the issue of statism. One of the ways that we solve this problem is by solving other problems, because they're all related. If you were to draw a chart of the average income brought into the family economy by working wives, starting back forty years ago, and if you were to draw another chart of the increase in the tax burden on the family starting forty years ago, you would think you had drawn one chart. They are absolutely right on track with each other.

Say that again.

The growth of the income by having the wife work has grown at exactly the same rate and is exactly the same number—

The same amount of money . . .

. . . as the growth of the tax burden on the family, which

means this: Our wives are going out to work to serve the state.

Well, R. C., I wish every Christian parent in America could listen to this series or read this book. I was instructed by it, and it's a delight for me to be instructed by my own son. And again, I wish that I would have known when you were a little tyke what you've taught me since. Again, I don't think that it's your desire—and it's certainly not mine—to put a guilt trip on anybody.

No.

That's not the point. I think parents in a godly home can turn the world upside down and that God has given us a mission field and a platform for influencing this world for the kingdom's sake.

It is an incredible opportunity. It is God's engine for building His kingdom.

Could you clarify the meaning of the term *covenant*, since throughout your lectures you talk about the covenant family, the covenant of redemption, how relationship to the church is a covenant, and so on? Can you just give us a little bit of explanation about that?

I can try. Covenant, as I said, is so central and so important to our understanding of all of the Bible and our relationships that it's very difficult to narrow it down. But to answer it quickly, basically the covenant is a series of obligations. God comes to man and says, "This is what I want you to do. This is what you're required to do. And I'm going to agree to do this." When He makes promises to Abraham or when He speaks to Adam and Eve in the garden, there's a series of agreements. And included with that are sanctions for obedience or disobedience.

Let me interrupt you. You say, first of all, there are obligations.

Yes.

And then you said promises.

Yes. Because God promises to do particular parts . . .

All right. Now when God promises to do something . . .

It's an obligation.

Well, was He obligated to promise it in the first place?

No, absolutely not. One of the things that we emphasized in this series is that what we miss about covenant when we look at it in terms of contract is that it's not negotiated, that when God comes and essentially makes the deal, first, He makes the deal in grace . . .

Right.

And second, if we obey and He blesses us, that is broader grace. So it's all grace. God doesn't have an obligation to promise to do something for us.

But once He makes the promise . . .

Then He does have an obligation based on His own character . . .

. . . and His integrity.

Right.

And that's the basis of our whole relationship with Him.

Absolutely.

Because we have a God who's made promises to us that we don't deserve.

Right.

But once He makes those promises, He keeps His word.

Yes, He does.

And we're supposed to reflect that in our own relationships.

Absolutely. And we are to keep our word and be in obedience to Him in all the obligations that He gives us, not only in relationship to Him—He also gives us obligations among each other. That's what we've talked about—husbands and wives and children have obligations among each other.

So we have a covenant with God.

Right.

But we also have covenants with each other.

Which is a part of our covenant with God because God gives us the covenants with each other.

Okay. You said a moment ago, when I interrupted, that there are obligations, there are promises, there's an agreement here between two or more parties.

Right.

But you also said covenants have sanctions.

Right.

Now, that's one of those fifty-cent words. What do you mean by sanctions?

Well, God comes and says, "If you keep My covenant, here are all kinds of blessings that I will bestow upon you." In fact, if you want to reduce God's covenants with man down to their bottom line, it's this: "Obey Me and you will be blessed. Disobey Me and you will be cursed."

And those are the exact words that the Old Testament writer, in Deuteronomy, uses: blessings and curses. And our whole understanding of the cross is based on that, isn't it?

Right. In fact, the cross is, in a sense, almost an addendum to this fundamental covenant that we disobeyed.

Right.

But Jesus is cursed.

So Jesus obeys.

Christ bears the curse . . .

. . . that we deserve.

Right.

That's because on the cross Jesus receives the negative covenant sanction . . .

Right.

. . . of His people . . .

True.

. . . who disobeyed God.

Right.

So, we even understand the cross in terms of the covenant.

Exactly. But in His life of total obedience, He earns the blessings, and these are imputed to us, and so we receive His blessings. The wonderful thing about the Gospel is that it doesn't undo this fundamental covenant but rather fulfills it and fits within it, so that God is both just and justifier. God keeps His promise, in terms of His own integrity, by sending the curse on Jesus and by granting us the rewards.

You just quoted a very famous man, the apostle Paul . . .

Yes, I did.

. . . in Romans 3, where Paul says, when he's talking about our redemption in the Gospel, that God is both just and the justifier. You know what, R. C.? I think that if we really understood that one sentence—that God is both just and justifier—it would have a profound impact on our understanding of the whole scope of the Christian faith.

Absolutely.

Now, here's another question that came from our audience. How does this covenant family series apply to grandparents?

Well, my book Family Practice *includes a chapter that I wrote seven years ago entitled "A Thirty-Year-Old Child," in which I addressed this. I asked the question, "What is the obligation of a grown child toward his or her parents?" And I talked about how parents, older parents who have older children, have a role of leadership to fulfill. If you look in*

Scripture, you see that God's covenant expands. You see that God makes covenant with Adam and Eve. Then, as we move forward, He makes covenant with Noah and his wife and his three sons and their wives. And then He makes covenant with Abraham, and Abraham becomes the clan. If you remember, when Abraham goes out to rescue Lot, quite a few people help him. Abraham serves as the patriarch of a clan. And, of course, so later does his son, Isaac. And it moves forward that way until finally Israel becomes a nation.

Well, what I would like to see, and what I think the Scripture presents for us, is an image for older men and women who have children, who become grandparents. They serve in that role of patriarch and matriarch. And their function is this: Their duty is to maintain a kind of consistency and obedience in the broader family while recognizing the absolute authority of the husband over the local family. So it becomes a sort of advisory role. And that means that I, as a grown man with my own family, have a duty. When I need counsel, to whom do I go? I go to you, which I'm sure a lot of other people would like to be able to do. I go to you because you are the patriarch of the clan. But if you say, "R. C., you must buy this house and sell that house," I have the authority and the freedom to say, "Thank you for your counsel, but I'm not going to do that."

What?

I will weigh your statement, and I need to weigh it—to take it very seriously. Look at it this way. We've talked in our discussion on the children about two verses that I teach my children: "Children, obey your parents in the Lord," and "Honor your father and your mother." Now, these two words "honor" and "obey" are definitely related. And I have a duty, as long as I'm under your covenantal authority, before

I establish my own authority as a man, to obey. And when that ends, I continue to have the duty to honor. Now, I want to say something else I didn't get a chance to say earlier about that. As we're working in our families, trying to affirm these covenants and to honor our parents, one of the things that parents need to do to help their children learn to honor and obey them is to watch carefully how they speak about their own parents—children will reflect the model that their parents have. If my children see me speak respectfully and honorably about you and your wife, my mother, then they're going to learn this is part of what those verses mean. If that is passed on, they're going to learn more powerfully to honor and respect me and my wife, your daughter-in-law.

R. C., I have a little different question, but related to this. Somebody raised, I thought, a poignant question: "When I was a young, married person and rearing our children, my wife and I weren't Christians. We didn't become Christians until after our kids were grown. So we did not raise our children in a Christian home. We did not raise them in the nurture and admonition of the Lord. And now our children are grown. Now what?"

Well, I think that brings to mind a bit of wisdom that a pastor who lives near me gave me one time. He was asked a very complicated question, and his answer was, "Sin complicates things." That is poignant. It is also heartbreaking. It's almost like the situation that Paul deals with when a grown man and a grown woman are married, and the wife becomes a believer, but her husband doesn't. What does Paul say to do? "Obey your husband. Submit to him as much as you can. Don't harass him. Don't fuss at him. And maybe, in God's providence and in God's grace, that might win him." So if parents become Christians later in life, what they should do

is the same thing they should do with other unrelated unbe-
lievers. They ought to model and reflect the godly, biblical
life. They should tell their grown children the Gospel, tell
them, "This is what's happened to us." And they should pray
that God would, through their example, lead their grown
children into the kingdom.

Okay. Now, one of the things that we're interested in is
establishing family traditions. I detect, in the culture in which
we live today, a growing antipathy toward tradition and tra-
ditionalism. We are very much a popular culture that lives for
the moment, in the here and now, and we tend to despise out-
moded traditions. We've seen *Fiddler on the Roof* and what
happens when traditions crumble and decay and so on. And
we also know that in biblical terms, Jesus was strongly critical of the scribes and Pharisees because they replaced the
Word of God with the traditions of men. Many Christians,
therefore, conclude that traditions are bad. And yet in the
New Testament Paul speaks about the *paradosis*, that which
has been given over, that which he received from the Lord,
which is what we call the apostolic tradition. There is a tradition that has its roots and basis in God.

Right.

And it's that tradition that you are talking about with the
shema. The parents have the responsibility to instruct their
children in the divine tradition.

Right.

Now, how do you do that? And what kind of traditions
do you have in your house that reinforce the divine tradition?

Well, I think that one of our bad traditions in America is
that we have this vision of child-rearing that is, in essence,
consumeristic. That is, too many parents think their job as a
parent is to lay before their children all the options there are

and hope and pray that they choose the right one, which is the exact opposite of what the shema *teaches and what Paul teaches in Ephesians 6. We're not called, as parents, to lay out these choices before our children. We are to put them on this path and lay the path down for them. And traditions are a part of doing that.*

Now what kind of practical traditions can we do? I think one thing we do in our family—you might call it a tradition, or you might just call it a good habit—is, we practice family worship in our home. In one sense that's not a complicated thing, though it's a little bit too involved to give a deep explanation of what we do. But it involves memorizing Scripture, and it involves memorizing the Westminster Shorter Catechism, which is our tradition. We're Presbyterian, but more than that, it's our tradition because we believe it's what the Bible teaches. We do singing and praying, and we open the Word, and I give little thirty-second sermons after every little passage that I read. But I want to be careful that we don't turn family worship into a means to an end. You know, the first question of the Shorter Catechism is, "What is the chief end of man?" "The chief end of man is to glorify God and to enjoy Him forever." When we're gathered together as a family for worship, that's what we're together for. So, whatever else comes out of it is just icing. And that includes things like helping them understand their identity. This is what we are. We are worshipers. We're not people who go out and do our own thing six days a week and for one hour on Sunday morning become this other thing. Rather, this is what we always are. And, of course, the teaching that we are instilling in them is what we affirm, what we believe. We teach them also, in a wonderful way, by what we sing. I have a friend who teaches on worship, and he says, "We think chil-

dren want to learn the children's songs—'Jesus Loves Me,' 'The B-I-B-L-E,' and all that—because they love them. And you know why they love them? Because that's what we teach them. If we teach them the hymns of the faith, they'll love those."

You have a video of Darby, my oldest, when she's four and in bed. Denise videotaped her bedroom door because we didn't want to go in there and disturb her. She was lying in bed singing "Holy, Holy, Holy" or "A Mighty Fortress Is Our God" or "Amazing Grace" just for fun because this is what she's learned and because, again, that places her in a tradition or in a covenant community that's broader than even our family. We're a part of the church of Jesus Christ, and this is what we do. So, there are a lot of things you can do to instill in your children this vision of what they are. We've talked so much about demographics, that their identity is not only not their particular age or gender or whatever. Their identity is part of this family, but it's bigger than that too. Their identity is that they're part of the church of Jesus Christ.

R. C., I don't want to put you on the hot seat here and create a controversy for you, but . . .

But you will.

Yeah, but I'm going to because one of the most important and richest traditions that we have in the church is the celebration of the Lord's Supper.

Yes.

I know that in our ecclesiastical tradition, the majority report is opposed to paedo-communion—that is, including children at the Lord's Table. And there's a whole case for that as you're aware. But there's also a minority report in Reformed theology that favors paedo-communion. And you stand in the minority group, I think.

Yes, I do.

Without giving a defense of that, apart from that whole controversy, isn't it important for us to help introduce our children to the broader traditions of the church?

Yes. And one of the ways that we do that—and this might be a more controversial thing—one of the ways that we do that in our family and in our church is by having our children in church with us. We come together as families into the sanctuary of God, and we worship together as families. And that again tells them not to go down the hall to go do such and such because of demographics; rather, we're going to worship together as families, because that's a part of your identity. We want you to participate, and it's not a burden, for goodness sake. It's a joyful thing. I love it when we have visitors in our church, and we stand up to sing a song, and I'm in the pulpit, and I see their eyes get like saucers, and they turn around because they've heard my little children and the other little children, as young as two and three years old, belting out the songs, singing with us the Apostles' Creed or the Nicene Creed or reciting together the liturgy of our church. And the visitors can't believe it. But this is what our children are. We're a part of this broader thing, and when we come to the Table, whether our children can eat or not, we teach them. In our church, we teach the children and the adults that here God's people are all together—all of God's people gathered before Christ's throne. We're all there as one body. My children know that in a sense they're there with Martin Luther. They're there with John Calvin. They're there with Father Abraham. All of us are gathered together. It's like coming, and there's your great-great-great-great grandfather at the Table. You're there with your great-grandfather, your father, and so on—we're all there together. And that again gives our children this vision, this identity, of what they are.

As you mentioned in your comments about the four institutions of individual, family, church, and state, we are perhaps one of the most individualistic cultures in the history of the world. And that's utterly foreign to the biblical culture. The biblical culture has a principle of corporate solidarity that's completely foreign to the culture in which we live today. So when the Philippian jailer says, "What must I do to be saved?" Paul says, "Believe in the Lord Jesus Christ, you and your whole household."

Right.

He just assumed this was not an individualistic experience for the jailer.

God makes covenants with families.

Well, let me ask you the next question. What books or programs do you recommend? What helps are there? A lot of people say, "I want to raise my children in a godly home. I want to be a godly parent. I want to take on these responsibilities. I feel guilty that I don't do more than I do, but the truth be told, I don't know how. How can you teach me? What kind of literature or help can you give me?"

There are many outstanding materials out there, more than in past ages. That's one of the things that's exciting about the age we live in—as the culture gets nastier and nastier and gets distinct from the church, more and more people begin to say, "Well, no, we can't do that." And they go back to the Scriptures and say, "What are we called to do?" And God has raised up so many godly teachers in our age to answer that. There are wonderful books out there by Douglas Wilson. He's done a whole series of books on the family. And his wife, Nancy Wilson, has written two books for wives. The

Fruit of Her Hands *and* Praise Her in the Gates *are both good books. Doug has written a book on child-rearing called* Standing on the Promises, *which is very much along the lines of what we're talking about. He has authored a book on marriage called* Reforming Marriage, *and also a wonderful book on courtship, which is something that the church is beginning to recover from her history, that looks at the marrying of our children in a more covenantal, familial way, called* Her Hand in Marriage.

There are other wonderful men and teachers out there as well, writing on child-rearing and discipline. Ted Tripp and his brother Paul have both written good books. Age of Opportunity *is one of them.* Shepherding a Child's Heart *is another really good one. There are also very good materials out there for family worship, the best of which, I think, is* Tabletalk *magazine. You know, just a few years ago we made what on one hand was a very small change and on the other a very large one in* Tabletalk, *when the page that introduces the daily Bible studies began to list some songs for families to sing together and some catechism to memorize, so our readers can do this together as a family. There's also a wonderful book called* Family Worship *by my friend Kerry Ptacek, published by Greenville Press. And that's just a handful of things that are very helpful and that have helped me.*

Well, let me ask you this. Spiritual leadership rests on the father. If there's a rebellious teenage child in the home of a minister, how should the father's role in the church be handled? You know that one of the qualifications for elders or ministers, according to 1 Timothy, is that they must rule their own households well. We see in the Old Testament what happened when Eli failed to discipline his sons—God took Eli and his sons.

Right.

And then when the sons of Aaron offered strange fire on the altar, God consumed them. Let me also mention here—I know this is a tangent, but my daughter, your sister, who's a grown woman, still is very uncomfortable when people say, "You're the minister's daughter."

Yes, she is.

You know about this spotlight that's put on ministers' kids. You grew up as a minister's child. What about this?

Well, I think we shouldn't focus the attention on the child because that's not what the passages in Timothy are dealing with. They're dealing with the parent and the parent's obligation. Now, on the issue of what to do with the pastor who has a rebellious teenager, I'm not ready to make a definitive stand on that issue, but I will say this: The vast majority of the evangelical church is way off on this because they completely ignore it. This is an important question. And we need to at least move somewhere toward asking the question. We need to move toward saying, "Okay, now what? Obviously something needs to happen here, but what is it?" Whether or not that means automatic defrocking, I'm not ready to say. I don't know because I learned from you that these qualifications are general, paradigmatic, that they're the ideal, which means that . . .

Nobody fulfills all of them perfectly.

Right. But that doesn't mean that failure to fulfill them is a matter of indifference, does it?

That's exactly right.

I do think the issue needs to be weighed much more carefully, much more heavily, and it's not just for pastors, what we call teaching elders, it's also for ruling elders. Our tendency in the American evangelical church is to choose ruling elders principally on the basis of success in busi-ness—prominent people in the community. And that's not on the list.

But there are situations where parents can be very godly people, do what they're supposed to do, and the child still maintains a rebellious spirit.

Right.

But the question is, is that rebellion because of a parental negligence or not? If it *is* a matter of negligence, then that does have bearing upon the qualifications of the person to be in a position of spiritual leadership.

Which means that we need to have a standard for what looks like negligence and what doesn't look like negligence. And I'm afraid that we're a long way from an appropriate standard. I mean, we think that if the father hasn't com-pletely abdicated his responsibilities, if he isn't a drunkard or doesn't beat the children, then he's a godly father. That's not enough. We need to raise that standard and then apply it in those situations. And I agree that it can happen that some-one can do well and the child still rebels. And by the way, someone who does do well also fails. No one is a perfect par-ent. But we need to have some sense of what the standard is, and those who don't meet it need to be removed from office and learn what this means. Or maybe to some degree it depends on the situation, I don't know. But I do think it can disqualify somebody.

Obviously, no one is a perfect parent, I agree with that. Have you ever met anybody that you thought came close to that?

Absolutely.

That's what I wanted to hear.

I'm just teasing. I appreciate your response to these ques-

tions because many people have them. You've touched a raw nerve, not in the sense of creating pain, but you've touched something where we feel that there's something really wrong in the lives of Christians and in the lives of the church. And you've set before us the distinction between the culture of this world and the culture of God.

Postscript

As with so many other biblical truths, our problem isn't so much what we haven't learned, but what we have learned and forgotten. We all know, for instance, that children last forever, while the toys that clutter our lives will all rust. But we still find ourselves hungering for the transient, for the vacuous. This reflects the first front line of the war we have already written about. The battle between the seed of the woman and the seed of the serpent is most fierce where it is closest to us, in the battle between the old man and the new, between our redeemed nature and our sin nature.

That we often fail in this battle, that we often forget the centrality of our families, is no reason to shirk the battle. Rather it should drive us to gird up our loins like men. There is, however, a decided difference between girding up our loins and seeking to pick ourselves up by our bootstraps. The difference is in our prayers. A bootstrap mentality is prideful and ineffective. But the most effective posture for raising and leading a godly family is on our knees.

We are not only to be prophetic to our families, bringing the Word of God to bear on their lives, but we are to be priestly. That is, we are to bring our families before the throne of God. When we who are husbands and fathers feel the weight of our responsibilities, we must cry out to our Father for strength and wisdom. There is no greater power in the work of sanctifying our families than prayer.

In like manner, when we recognize that we have failed, whether it is a brief failure or a lifetime of failure, the Scripture gives us clear direction—we must repent. Over the years as I have taught on the family, I have had people get angry. I have had people express great gratitude. I have had, particularly among unmarried women and women married to unbelieving or weak husbands, many express longing. But nothing touches my heart more than those who respond with regret. Many parents who are past the season in life where they are raising children recognize that they had failed to see their task in truly biblical terms. And many, with tears in their eyes, concede that they are reaping what they have sown.

Here we especially must remember our ultimate family. We are all together the bride of Christ, who even now intercedes for us before the Father. And we are, in Christ, joint heirs with Him. We have an unspeakable privilege—He allows us to be called His children. This is why, and the context in which, we repent, all of us, for our failures. None of us is a perfect parent. All of us have missed opportunities. All of us have regrets. And all of us, if we are in Christ, have our sins covered.

That is our joy. We have been adopted into the only non-dysfunctional family in the universe. And He who has begun a good work in us has promised to bring us to perfection. If our children are grown, let us pray that He would cover our failures and empower us to be godly parents and, God willing, godly grandparents. If our children are still with us, then we can pray that He will empower us to do right by our children. Whatever our circumstances, whether we have just begun the race, whether we ran poorly, or whether we have run well, all of this is in our Father's almighty hands. And so we can be at peace, remembering that Christ never fails. We can be confident that we are, indeed, bound for glory.

INDEX